Golden-Crowned Kinglets

TREETOP NESTERS OF THE NORTH WOODS

Golden-Crowned Kinglets

TREETOP NESTERS OF THE NORTH WOODS

ROBERT GALATI

Illustrated by Colleen Helgeson Nelson
With a foreword by Joseph J. Hickey

Iowa State University Press / Ames

Manufactured in the United States of America
∞ This book is printed on acid-free paper.

First edition, 1991

Library of Congress Cataloging-in-Publication Data

Galati, Robert.
    Golden-crowned kinglets: treetop nesters of the north woods / Robert Galati : illustrated by Colleen Helgeson Nelson : with a foreword by Joseph J. Hickey.— 1st ed.
      p.   cm.
    Includes index.
    ISBN 0-8138-0394-2 (alk. paper)
    1. Golden-crowned kinglet.   I. Title.
QL696.P27G34 1991   90-37373
598.8—dc20

Robert Galati is a retired science teacher. He and Carlyn, his wife, have been avid birders since the late 1940s, concentrating their research on the golden-crowned kinglet in the 1950s.

To Carlyn

I am greatly indebted to my wife, Carlyn, for the tremendous amount of time she spent sharing observations with me through five seasons of study. She shared mosquitoes and other insect pests, cold and hot weather, wind and rain storms, long hours in the treetops, never complaining as the secrets of the golden-crowned kinglet began to unravel. Had it not been for her, the study would have been greatly restricted.

CONTENTS

FOREWORD

THIS BOOK is one of the most intimate accounts of nesting birds that has been written. Its subject, the golden-crowned kinglet, proves to be among the most fearless of all North American songbirds, and the descriptions of its reaction to inquisitive ornithologists are a sheer delight.

That so small a bird should annually lay a clutch of nine eggs is, indeed, notable. That it should regularly attempt a second clutch of virtually the same size is astonishing. Clearly, the kinglet is no ordinary bird.

In many ways, this tiny creature will always be among the more difficult species to study in the wild. During its nesting season, however, it is tied to a definite territory. Although this area is surprisingly large for so small a bird, it offers the ornithologist the best opportunity to observe this very active and somewhat elusive species. This book describes the successful observation of the kinglet in these circumstances. It is a story of tenacity, patience, and imaginative techniques. The result is a substantial contribution to our knowledge of a seldom-studied species.

But the book is more than just science. It is a fascinating collection of the kind of stories that seldom find their way into print. Because of the cost and publishing philosophy of scientific journals, most such stories are told around the dinner table and forgotten. This book is an exception, as Bob Galati takes readers behind the scenes of both the kinglets and their observers and tells the stories that make the scientific data come alive.

Joseph J. Hickey, *Professor Emeritus*
Department of Wildlife Ecology
University of Wisconsin-Madison

ACKNOWLEDGMENTS

I EXPRESS APPRECIATION to William H. Marshall and the late T. Shantz-Hansen, who made facilities at the University of Minnesota's Forestry and Biological Station available to us, and to Walter Nelson, maintenance foreman, who directed construction of our four towers and supplied us with tools, equipment, and supplies that enabled us to reach our other nests.

I thank Joseph J. Hickey, under whose direction and guidance I initiated my study, and John T. Emlen, Jr., and the late S. Charles Kendeigh, who gave me further direction and guidance. I also give sincere thanks to these ornithologists for critical advice. In addition, I thank John Emlen for his interest and encouragement in helping to get this manuscript published.

I thank Colleen Helgeson Nelson for spending many hours at the top of one of our towers sketching the development of nestlings, and for her paintings and sketches of the adult kinglets.

I thank Alvah Peterson for identifying insects that were collected from the kinglets.

I am grateful to William E. Dunton, who read the manuscript several times and asked for clarification of many points. I also appreciate his typing and retyping early versions of this manuscript. I am ever grateful to Susan Hickey Nehls for her editing and typing of my book and for preparing its index.

Golden-Crowned Kinglets

TREETOP NESTERS OF THE NORTH WOODS

1

How We Got Started

BACK IN MY BOYHOOD as I was thumbing through a book on birds, I saw a colored plate of a golden-crowned kinglet. The tiny bird immediately caught my fancy, and I wondered where I could go to see it. I learned that it belonged to a genus called *Regulus,* "little king," in recognition of the crown of yellow or orange on top of its head. I also learned that it is, except for the hummingbird, the smallest of our American birds. Little did I know then that this miniature creature was to be the subject of intensive personal research in later years.

In the summer of 1954 I enrolled in an ornithology course at the University of Minnesota's Forestry and Biological Station, located in Itasca State Park. Dr. J. J. Hickey, visiting ornithologist from the University of Wisconsin-Madison, was my advisor. For my course problem I chose to find a golden-crowned kinglet nest, and learn something about kinglet behavior. I discovered from existing literature that I had chosen a bird about which little was known; in fact, only six nests had ever been reported in Minnesota. There was no information about territorial behavior, length of incubation, nestling state, or fledgling period.

As I walked near the main entrance of the campus on a number of occasions, I heard kinglets singing. After observing a pair over a period of four days, I located my first kinglet nest in a white spruce, 27 feet from the ground. I watched the female enter a hanging cluster of twigs on the underside of a branch near its tip. Even with binoculars, I could barely make out a partial outline of the nest, so the station's maintenance department built a 30-foot tower from which I could observe the kinglets' behavior. There were nine eggs in the nest. This was to be the lowest and easiest to locate of all the nests eventually found.

Because my other course work took time away from the kinglet study, I enlisted the services of my wife, Carlyn, and together we started the project by alternating observation periods. By the end of the summer, we had only been able to observe one pair of kinglets. We were left with so many un-answered questions that we decided to return the following season and continue our observations. We ended by studying the breeding biology of the golden-crowned kinglet not only in 1954 but also 1955, 1956, 1957, and 1960. Approximately 3,800 hours were spent observing these birds throughout the various activities of their nesting cycles. Nineteen kinglet nests involving 13 different breeding pairs were found during the study.

From time to time, people would ask us why we spent so much time studying a silly little bird that most people didn't know existed. I answered by asking an equally silly question, "Why do people climb mountains? Because they are there."

We chose a bird about which little was known. It was fun being pioneers in learning about a friendly little creature that allowed us to delve into its deepest secrets. No one had ever attempted to do an in-depth study of a bird that nested so high in the trees. I always wanted to contribute my bit to the field of ornithology, and here was my chance.

The technical findings of our study have been published in Galati and Galati (1985). What appears here is the more personal aspect of the story, together with a scattering of ob-servations on how kinglets managed to survive and rear their young in the treetops of Minnesota's northern coniferous forests.

Studying kinglets. There are many disadvantages to choosing the golden-crowned kinglet as a subject for study, but these are abundantly offset by a number of advantages: both sexes remain in the established territory during the breeding season, the males can be approached and followed by listening to their distinctive vocalizations, and males tend to perch regularly in the same trees and at approximately the same height each day during egg laying and incubation. Any bird-watcher posted at these places at the right season can expect to hear or see a kinglet before many minutes have passed. Once a nest has been found, the confiding ways and parental persistence of both male and female offer joys no bird-watcher can fail to admire.

When we finally found nests and erected our observation towers, the birds freely allowed us to part the branches and twigs that hid their nests from view and observe them from only a foot away. All females at nests that were under intensive study allowed us to reach into the nest and pick them up. The female, and occasionally the male, visited us in the blind, and even landed on us at times. When the adults blocked our view of the number of nestlings they were feeding, we could push them aside with a finger without unduly disturbing them.

Once, when we tried prodding a female to leave her nest so that we could weigh the young, she refused to go. I attempted removing her with my hand, but she held onto the nest's lining with her toes. She did the same thing the following day when we again tried to remove her. Females at other nests had to be forcibly removed by hand when they refused to leave the nest; on numerous occasions, they would fly into the blind and hop around the scale while we took the desired observations and weights.

Artist Colleen H. Nelson spent much time in the blind making paintings of the adults, nestlings, and nest. The parent kinglets made numerous visits into the blind, eyed her up and down, and then proceeded to hop around and survey all the supplies and equipment she had. At times they landed on her as well. When we removed nestlings at different ages so she could make ink sketches of their day-by-

Kinglets are unconcerned by the extreme closeness of observers.

day development, neither parent ever hesitated to fly into the blind, feed the nestlings, and again hop about, surveying the activity.

On occasion we invited other ornithologists and friends to watch the kinglets feed their nestlings. As soon as the adults returned from a feeding visit, they immediately flew in to look over the new visitors. Our visitors were thrilled when one of the adults would sometimes land on them. It appeared that if we tolerated the visitors, it was all right with the kinglets.

There are reports from others that kinglets may be quite tame at times other than during the nesting season. Church (1927) found them very friendly in her Great Neck, Long Island, garden. On October 15, she followed a group closely enough to stroke several of them. They showed no fear when she patted them and stroked their crest and parted their wings. They sat on her hands and lit on her coat. Wood (1884) was on a boat in Lake Michigan, which was invaded by 8 or 10 kinglets. They made their way into a cabin and perched on the heads of passengers and on dishes set out on a table. He caught some flies, which they readily took from his hand with a quick flutter. He caught several birds, and even when in his hand, they seemed to show no fear but lay quiet and passive.

Marking birds and eggs. All eggs, nestlings, and adults at nests that were under intensive study were marked for individual identification with different colors of acetate-based paint. Adult females were dabbed with a paintbrush while they incubated or brooded the young. Males never brooded, so they were color marked when they fed their mates or nestlings. Because the males visited the nests less frequently than the females during the earlier stages of the nesting cycle and flew off each time their tail feathers were touched with the brush, it took several visits before there was enough color to identify them from a distance. Eggs were marked and weighed just after they were laid, and they were weighed again before they hatched so we could learn if there was weight loss. We marked the nestlings in order to follow the daily feather-tract development and weight increase of known individuals.

Nestlings had to be frequently recolored because the adults would peck off the paint. One time Carlyn tried to discourage the removal by pushing the female's bill away from the nestlings each time she would start pecking at the paint. It was to no avail—we finally had to put more color on the nestlings.

Color bands were used on the nestlings when their legs were sufficiently developed (12 to 14 days). The nestlings in our first nest (1954) were tagged with U. S. Fish and Wildlife Service aluminum bands. We had planned to resume our observations of the kinglets the following year and wanted to see if these young would return to the same area. Not one of the banded birds was seen the following year.

Building tree towers and platforms. Nests under intensive study were observed from blinds built atop tall towers or lashed to rough platforms in trees next to the one that had the nest. Four towers (8, 30, 50, and 53 feet in height) were constructed for us. In addition, three tree platforms were built in trees next to nesting trees, and two platforms were put directly in the nesting trees.

Eleven nests were reached by using spikes that had been driven into tree trunks. A path was cut through the branches to within a few feet below the nest so we would not have to push through a maze of branches to reach the nests. One aluminum tree pole with alternating lateral rungs approximately 1 foot apart was used to reach a nest that was 60.5 feet from the ground.

The blinds were made out of heavy canvas and were dark green, blending well with the surrounding foliage. They were square, measuring 4 feet by 4 feet. The back section consisted of one flap that was attached only at the top. The bottom corners had straps that could be tied to the straps of the

This 53-foot tower was one of the three tall towers constructed for us to observe kinglets high in the treetops.

Tree platforms were used to observe kinglets when a neighboring tree was strong enough to support us.

two side sections. The tops of our towers and tree platforms had four corner posts over which we draped our blinds. The front of the blind had three vertical slits with zippers so that more than one person could view nest activities.

Taking incubation temperature. In 1956 we attempted to measure the temperature that an incubating female supplied to her eggs. A thermometer was pushed upward through the bottom of the nest so the tip of it rested about level with the top of the eggs in the center of the nest. The female had just left after a 21-minute period of attentiveness. When she returned to resume incubation, she sensed something was not completely right. She raised and lowered herself repeatedly, making quarter and half turns, shaking from side to side, and then pecking the thermometer tip.

When she finally settled down, the thermometer reading rose from 95°F to 105°F within a minute. The temperature dropped to 92°F when the thermometer was lowered so that its tip was approximately level with the underside of the lowest eggs. The temperature rose to 104°F when I raised the thermometer tip to the top of the eggs again. The nest retained the heat quite efficiently after the female left for short periods.

Sampling the food brought to the nest. A cross section of food items was taken at three different nests by removing insects with forceps from the adults' bills just be-

fore they fed the nestlings. My first attempt at stealing food from the bill of a kinglet was during the initial nesting cycle of a pair we were observing. The female arrived with a large caterpillar and a number of tiny, winged insects. When I made a motion toward her bill, she froze and allowed me to take the larva. But before I could put it in a vial of alcohol, she flew to the forceps, momentarily hovered, retrieved the larva, and then quickly returned to the nest rim. I removed the caterpillar from her bill again and succeeded in putting it in the vial. She fed the remaining insects to the nestlings and left. When the male arrived, I took some insects from his bill. He crested (elevated and spread his crown feathers) and flew off but quickly returned and fed three nestlings the remaining insects.

Several more attempts were made to take food from this pair that day and the following one. At times I was able to take food from them without a struggle, but at other times before I could take any, the adults would succeed in feeding the young. They dodged the forceps and fed so quickly after they got used to my food stealing that it was more difficult to take food from their bills.

I also attempted taking food from another pair of kinglets during that pair's first nesting. The male arrived with a bill full of insects, and I pulled out one larva. He immediately hopped to the opposite side of the nest. When I tried to take another insect, he quickly dodged the forceps and fed a nestling. The next time he returned, I was unsuccessful because he avoided the forceps and fed his nestlings. Three more attempts at stealing food from the male were unsuccessful.

A path was cut to this nesting site. We used one section of an aluminum tree pole to reach the lower branches; then we stepped on the branches until we got to the platform.

A tree pole was used to reach this tree platform 60.5 feet from the ground.

When he returned for the fifth time, I made no attempt to take any food items, having failed four consecutive times. Seven gaping mouths greeted him, but he did not feed them. He appeared to be waiting for me to take some food—or at least to try. When I finally did, he appeared stunned and didn't move a muscle. After remaining still for about 10 seconds, he flew off and returned immediately. I made another try, but he evaded the forceps and fed the nestlings.

My first two attempts to take insects from his mate failed

14

too, as she avoided the forceps and fed the nestlings. On her third visit, I succeeded in pulling a larva out of her bill. She followed it into the blind, fluttering and hovering in front of my face like a hummingbird. Then she landed on the blind's zipper. As I was putting the insect into the vial, she hopped around it and then flew out.

When this same pair nested a second time, I collected more items from them. One larva that I took from the female changed hands five times. After the fourth exchange, I was able to get it into the vial before she took it back. Each time she flew to the forceps and hovered hummingbird-fashion before retrieving the larva.

After the male had dodged the forceps on several visits in succession, I put my hand over the nest opening as he approached. He made three attempts to feed the young by poking his bill between my slightly spread fingers. He also flew into the blind once, and hopped around the vial as I put the insect into it.

Controlling predators. Predators were removed from around nests under intensive study. Red squirrels were the principal offenders, and we usually shot them if and when they came within a few feet of the nest. Red squirrels forage for cones, which tend to be heavily concentrated in the crowns of spruce and fir trees, the sites chosen by kinglets for their nests. We did not attempt to control predators in nesting areas where only spot checks were made daily.

Team studying. Since two of us were involved in the kinglet study, one of us generally observed behavioral activities at the nest, while the other observed kinglet activities from the ground within the pair's territory. Observations were also conducted in other areas where nests had been found and territories determined. Observers were in direct communication with one another at each nesting site when a pair started a second nest while they still had nestlings in the first nest.

Resuming studies in 1955.

Spring had started early in northern Minnesota when my wife and I returned on May 14, 1955, to spend our second season with the kinglets. All the snow had melted, and the forest was unusually dry for mid-May. Myriads of birds passed through en route to their northern nesting grounds. Already many different species of songbirds had settled in the park and set up territories. Their songs echoed through the forest, warning other birds of their own species to move on because they had squatters' rights.

The forestry and biological station campus was deserted except for the activities of the maintenance department. Walt Nelson, the foreman, and his crew were busy getting the station ready for the biology session that was to begin in another month. Dr. T. Schantz-Hansen, the station's director, had granted us permission to resume our studies at the station before it officially opened in mid-June.

Nest hunting and other problems.

We spent our first day wandering around the campus looking for kinglets but failed to hear or see any.

The following day found us east of the biology station in a mixed stand of white spruce; balsam fir; red, white, and jack pine; and paper birch. As we looked overhead, a feeling of defeat swept through us. The tree crowns were so close together that very little light penetrated, and our job was to find, in the dense green foliage above, a diminutive bird 3½ to 4 inches in length, with a drab olive-gray back and buffy undersides. It was not much consolation to know that the female kinglet had a conspicuous bright yellow crown stripe and the male an orange one bordered by yellow, because we would be viewing them from underneath.

> *One of the most difficult and time-consuming jobs was locating kinglet nests. It took us two weeks to find our second nest.*

It was like looking for a needle in a haystack, but we were fortunate in that our subject had a song, even though it was rather weak compared with that of other birds in the area. No sooner had we oriented ourselves to the area than the plaintive "tsee, tsee, tsee" call notes of the kinglet filtered through to us. After tripping over dead branches and getting slapped with an occasional dead twig, we managed to find the general area from whence the song came. It was very difficult to keep from falling into holes as we stumbled along with our eyes scanning the treetops. The periodic "tsee" notes seemed to come from the spruce-tamarack bog to the east, so we hurriedly made our way over to it.

A veritable obstacle course lay before us as we entered the bog. Numerous trees had been blown over in a windstorm, so it was almost impossible to make our way through the windfalls. We were about to turn back after making several unsuccessful attempts, when the kinglet sang again.

This time the song came from behind us. We scurried toward it and then stopped to listen for an encore. In a few minutes we were rewarded with more call notes, which seemed to come from directly overhead. Noticing a movement on a branch above, I quickly raised my binoculars and focused them on the spot. It was a kinglet preening itself on a dead twig near the trunk of a fir tree! As it preened the underpart of its left wing, I noticed a thin orange crown stripe. It was the male! He continued to sing and preen for almost 20 minutes.

Suddenly, three rapid "tsee" notes were emitted directly above him. The male spread his orange crest so that his crown looked as if it were on fire. He sang his full song and flew toward the west. We scrambled after him, determined not to let him out of our sight. He continued to sing as he flew from tree to tree. Above him we caught glimpses of another bird foraging in the treetops. It proved to be the female kinglet when we viewed it through our binoculars. The male did not join her but stayed at the lower level, giving his call notes at brief intervals.

I watched the female, and Carlyn watched the male. We thought maybe one of them would lead us to their nesting site. In a few minutes the female disappeared over the treetops, followed closely by the male. We stopped and listened for their song periodically as we walked in the same direction, hoping to hear their high-pitched "tsee" notes.

Once after we had stood quietly for a few minutes, an ovenbird came to within a few feet of us and bellowed, "Teacher! Teacher! Teacher!" His song drowned out all other bird songs and left us feeling a wee bit shaken. "Why didn't the kinglet have a loud song?" I queried.

As we were about to give up, we heard the kinglets once again. This time we found them on a branch just a few feet from the ground. The male foraged while the female begged for food. She opened her bill and fluttered her wings like young birds do when they beg for food. She kept up a continuous trill until she was fed. This behavior is thought to be a stimulus for nest building and other activities related to breeding. In a few minutes both kinglets flew to the southeast, leaving us in a muddle again. We continued to locate and then lose them at intervals.

As we hunted, we saw a pair of blackburnian warblers foraging in the trees. The female followed the male and begged for food also. They apparently had chosen the same area as the kinglets for nesting. Two red squirrels were seen feeding on cones in the crown of a balsam fir. Knowing they were not averse to eating bird's eggs or young, we wondered how many bird nests they would find.

Carlyn eventually decided that she had had enough kinglet stalking for one day. Her neck was sore from looking up so much, and her eyes were tired. I felt the same as she did, so we concluded our kinglet hunting for the day.

We were up and about the station at dawn the following morning. The phoebe, blackburnian and mourning warblers, red-eyed vireo, and chipping sparrow were among the early risers proclaiming their territorial rights. As we entered the kinglet area, we were greeted by the drumming of a ruffed grouse and the songs of a northern parula, solitary vireo, winter wren, ovenbird, and our subject of study, the golden-crowned kinglet.

My day's activities included two arduous, risky climbs in

We believed red squirrels, attracted to cones near kinglet nests, were the main predators of kinglets. Note the spruce cones behind the nest.

fir trees to points where the trunks narrowed to a mere inch. Behavior of the female kinglet had led us to believe that one of the crowns harbored her nest.

Carlyn's activities for the day almost put her out of action. While she was trailing the female and I, the male, I heard her scream. Thinking that she was being attacked by some forest creature, I quickly traced her whereabouts by her calls. She had fallen into a pit that a forestry student had dug a previous year in order to conduct an experiment.

She was unharmed but a little shaken. Her pride was injured more than anything else. She informed me that she was so intent on not losing sight of the female that she failed to watch where she was going, and before she realized it, the ground had opened up and swallowed her. At any rate, we lost sight of both the female and the male, so we started from scratch again.

The end of the day found us with aching necks, scratches, and bruises, and thoroughly exhausted. The kinglets had eluded us again.

As the days passed, we continued to stalk the kinglets. The mosquito population had increased to a point where they almost got the best of us. They seemed to thrive on the insect repellent with which we had drenched ourselves. I was sure that each swat of my face netted me at least 50 of the pesky parasites. In the meantime, more trees had been climbed, but none of them held a kinglet nest.

Just to the south of us was a bog covered mainly with black spruce. On several occasions we had heard kinglets singing from that direction, so we decided to hike along the La Salle Trail, which bordered the southern edge of the bog.

As we slowly hiked down the trail listening for kinglet songs, a ruffed grouse appeared suddenly from the brush, seized me by my right trouser leg with his bill, and began beating his wings vigorously. Since the beating caused me no pain, I let him have his way and for over 30 minutes he carried on with his attacks. After each attack he stepped back and eyed me intently while clucking and cocking his head from side to side as if to survey his handiwork. His attacks became more vigorous whenever I attempted to walk down

the trail. He desisted only after I stepped off the path and entered the heavy undercover. Such behavior, I learned, is not uncommon for this and several other species of the grouse family during the breeding season. It has earned them the name of fool hen in some areas.

In the days to follow I was treated in the same shabby way by my ruffed friend. One day he walked to the car and noticed his reflection in the hubcap. He attacked his image with his bill, feet, and wings. When I started to back the car, he flew onto the hood and attacked the windshield. As I backed the car, he attacked the window more vigorously. As I picked up speed, he slipped off and chased the car full speed and ran right past it.

We were to meet him again a few days later in the parking lot where he was attacking my hubcap tooth and nail. This type of behavior went on for two weeks.

One day I decided to get some motion pictures of his attacks, so I sent Carlyn ahead to see what would happen. The grouse eyed her quizzically, emitted clucking sounds, and walked along side of her without one attack. She walked by him repeatedly but still no reaction from him. I had her take over the camera and get some pictures of me as I walked by him, and lo and behold, without hesitation, he attacked me with a vengeance. I changed places with Carlyn again, but the most she got out of him was a few clucks and cocked heads. Apparently fair damsels are off limits to ruffed grouse.

We returned to our original hunting ground, determined to find the kinglets' nest. Two weeks had passed since we began our search.

At least we had discovered the boundaries of the pair's approximately six-acre territory. The male confined his ac-

We climbed many trees in vain, checking their crowns for nests after we saw the birds disappear into them and not come out.

tivities mostly to periodic singing on dead limbs 30 to 40 feet up in different trees within a stone's throw of a central point where we guessed the nest must be. Occasionally he would fly to the crowns to feed or to join the female, who was seldom seen except when foraging. We had several trees marked where we thought they might have a nest, but which one held it?

The female had disappeared into the foliage of several different balsam firs approximately 60 feet from the ground. In each case, almost 40 feet of dry, spindly limbs that were too thin to support human weight had to be contended with before foliage could be reached, and then the main trunk narrowed so rapidly that it would be risky to climb any further. After struggling up two trees to a point where I was risking my life, I temporarily abandoned the idea of climbing trees.

On May 26 at 7:40 A.M. during a slight rain, the male was seen singing 30 feet up in a fir on a dead limb. He had what looked like dried leaves hanging out of his bill. He sang for five minutes and then flew to the ground. He picked up a few more dry leaves, hopped to a dead log, and added some moss to his collection. After spending four minutes on the ground, he flew to the northeastern end of his territory and disappeared from sight. I tried frantically to follow him, but between the rain and heavy foliage, it was practically impossible.

This was the fourteenth day after we began observing the kinglet pair, and we finally got our first clue as to what they might be doing. We learned later that the easiest period to find a nest in the kinglet's nesting cycle is when it is in the process of constructing its nest or feeding nestlings. This is the easiest time because it is making numerous visits to the nesting site. Its visits are few and far between when it is laying eggs or incubating.

By observing the male collecting what looked like nesting material we concluded that the pair was building its nest, but we were to be proven wrong within the next hour. We visually followed the female to the top of a fir and watched her disappear into the west side. We kept our eyes fixed on the spot where she was last seen. We were finally rewarded with her reappearence a half hour later.

Now we felt certain that she had a nest there. She flew to the northwestern part of the territory with the male in hot pursuit. A few minutes later she returned to the fir and disappeared into the same cluster of foliage from which we had previously seen her emerge. I judged that her nesting site was approximately 60 feet from the ground. The tree was thin to begin with, and it tapered to practically nothing at the height where we expected to find the nest.

We went to the maintenance department for assistance. Walt Nelson decided that a tower was impractical, but he thought that it would be feasible to build a 50-foot ladder in 10-foot sections, hook a block and tackle to the first section, and tack each succeeding section on as the ladder was raised.

The first two ladder sections were nailed together and raised by hand. I chopped dead limbs for the first 20 feet and hooked up the block and tackle to the ladder.

The limbs proved to be a nuisance all the way up. The ladder could not be raised because of them, and one could not go beyond the ladder to chop them. Because of this problem, it was an all-day job just raising the ladder. The chain supporting the block had to be raised gradually while the slack in the line was taken up. When the last section of the ladder was nailed, we found that it was too short, so the ladder was raised another 7 feet and had to be lashed to the tree every 10 feet. The ladder and tree were quite shaky so they were guyed for safety.

As I climbed the shaky ladder, the male kinglet accompanied me, uttering his distress call. While I was combing the crown branches, the female joined the distressed male. When I searched the area from which she had flown, I finally found the nest—58 feet 10 inches from the ground. It was a cozy, globular-shaped construction completely hidden from view in the branches near the trunk of the tree and was composed of nesting materials that blended well with the fir needles. It housed nine tiny, cream-colored eggs. I could understand why few eyes had seen a kinglet's nest.

To observe nesting behavior from my shaky perch was impractical so I descended. As we returned to the station, the thought of lowering the nest came to mind. Dr. Bill Stull, an ornithologist from Delaware, Ohio, had arrived at the station in the meantime to do research on the chipping sparrow before his teaching duties were to begin. I consulted with him about lowering the nest, and he thought it would be worth a try but warned that the pair might desert the nest.

We returned to the nesting tree with Dr. Stull and Walt Nelson. The top of the tree ladder ended 3 feet below the kinglet nest. I nailed a board to one side of the ladder to extend it 2 feet above the nest, wired a pulley to the top of the ladder, ran a line ʰhrough the pulley, and lashed it around the trunk above the nest. The other end of the line extended to the ground. I then cut the trunk 7 feet from the treetop and 2 feet below the nest. It was my intention to lower that part of the treetop that contained the nest to a suitable level for observation.

Unfortunately, I had miscalculated. The line had been lashed too low and my treetop with its precious burden tipped precariously. I lunged out, grabbed the crown, and uprighted it just as the eggs were about to roll out of the nest. I had to use both hands to keep it in balance. My safety belt slack was taken up suddenly, and I found myself leaning away from the tree, which swayed and took on a decided bend. Only the ladder prevented the tree from snapping under my weight. As I continued my struggle to keep the treetop upright, Dr. Stull yelled for me to let the tree go, because it wasn't worth risking my life to save the nest.

I called back that I couldn't because it had taken us two weeks to find it and I didn't want to lose it. I thought about the distressed kinglets buzzing around me. It was I who had caused their nest to be in peril, and it was up to me to save it. They scolded me from the top of the tree while Dr. Stull continued with his pleas from the ground.

Walt could not bear to see me in my precarious position, so he left the scene muttering, "Let me know where to bury the body."

I was afraid that any movement on my part would cause

the ladder and tree to break. Periodically I made feeble attempts to get into position to move the line up, but my situation became more perilous with each attempt. For a while it looked as if I would have to release my hold on the tree and let the eggs roll out, but the sight of the distressed kinglets continued to spur me on. With much trepidation I resumed my efforts and finally succeeded in raising the line high enough for the tree to remain upright under its own weight.

I then lashed a pole with a pulley attachment to the tree and lowered the nest 15 feet. The female kinglet "tseed" excitedly and looked for it in the remaining foliage at the top. She was unable to find it over a 40-minute period, so I raised the top to the level of the remaining foliage. Within a few minutes she located the nest and resumed her incubation. I chopped all the foliage that remained below the cut and lowered the nest 10 feet. The female found her nest within two minutes. Three hours later I lowered the part containing the nest 10 more feet, and she found it immediately this time.

The following day the nest was lowered 10 more feet in the morning and another 10 feet in the afternoon. The female continued to follow its descent and incubate her eggs. On the third day the nest was lowered to within 8 feet from the ground and lashed securely to the tree trunk. To retard the foliage from drying out, the stem base was put in a bucket containing sand and water. An 8-foot tower was constructed and a green canvas blind was draped over the top for observing the birds.

On June 8, eight days after the nest had been found, we returned early in the morning to resume our observations and found the contents—eight nestlings and one egg—missing. Some predator had raided the nest! Nearby at the base of a neighboring tree were the suspects—two red squirrels.

With the loss of our nest it was back to ground zero. The day's end found us once again with sore necks, exhausted and dejected. Would we have to spend another two weeks finding out what the kinglets were up to?

To our great relief, early the following morning we found our marked pair building a nest at the eastern end of their territory approximately 200 feet from the original site. We were further comforted to see that they had chosen a branch of a tall, sturdy white spruce.

The tree ladder was transferred to a tree near the spruce by the especially cooperative maintenance department. A tree platform was partially built and raised, by means of a block and tackle, to the nest level. After securing the platform to the trunk, I completed its construction in the tree.

The tree holding the nest was approximately 90 feet high. The nesting site was located on the underside of a horizontal branch 11 feet from the trunk and 56 feet from the ground. The platform was funnel-shaped with its narrowest part emanating from the tree trunk. It was too shaky to walk on upright, so we crawled out on the catwalk on our hands and knees and cautiously made our way to the blind.

A tree platform was constructed in this tree directly across from a neighboring tree that housed the nest.

This tree platform, 56 feet up in a white spruce, was
constructed in the same tree that housed the nest.
The nest was located in the cluster of twigs in front of
the observer.

29

Once in the blind we felt much safer because we were not compelled to look below. We either sat with our legs crossed or lay on our sides during our observation periods. Occasionally we had to change positions due to leg, side, or back cramps.

Each movement caused the platform to sway. Although we knew that the wire supporting the platform was supposed to support a thousand pounds, we still felt uneasy. What if a strong wind came up? It was with much trepidation that we relieved one another each time.

From our shaky perch we were able to observe the kinglets constructing their second nest. They appeared to build it with a great deal of care. The female did most of the nest building while the male spent much of his time escorting her to and from it.

When their nest was almost completed, they deserted it. Disheartened, Carlyn continued her vigilance from the blind to see if they would return, while I followed the birds from the ground.

It was a joyous moment when we found the kinglets building their third nest the following morning. They had chosen a branch 50 feet up in a balsam fir, approximately 600 feet from their second nesting site. Their perseverance was matched only by that of the maintenance department, for Walt Nelson and his crew came to our rescue for the third time and built a 50-foot wooden tower, from which we could view kinglet activities in comfort.

Occasionally the pesky mosquitoes and the tiny black insects "no-see-ums" made their way to the top of our tower and entered the blind. We found it was worth our time and efforts to kill them since they did not frequent our aerie in an endless chain.

This was the first high tower built for us (50 feet high). There were no trees nearby that were strong enough to support a tree platform.

The kinglets completed their third nest in five days. The first egg was laid the next day, followed by an additional one each succeeding day until nine were laid. Occasionally the male visited the nest and fed the female during her long incubation periods.

Early one morning just after I had arrived to begin the day's observations, I heard thumping sounds below. Peeking out of the blind, I saw a red squirrel making his way up the tower. When he was about halfway up, he jumped off the tower to the nesting tree and continued his ascent until he came within a couple feet of the nest.

In the meantime, I had grabbed a stick and was ready to use it if necessary. As he began foraging on the nearby cones, his movements stimulated the young to gape for food. In a flash the red squirrel was at the nest's edge. The nestlings immediately cowered. Just as I was about to swing, he sensed my presence, leaped to a neighboring tree, and scurried down. In a few minutes the male kinglet returned, oblivious to what had just occurred, and fed the nestlings.

The red squirrel made another visit the next day, but I foiled his second attempt. From then until the nestlings fledged, my wife and I stood guard, starting our observations before the red squirrels became active each day, and continuing them until the squirrels retired for the night.

Surviving perils. Nature was not always kind to us up there. At times we were caught in our lofty perch during lightning and thunderstorms. Because it was imperative that our observation periods be conducted seven days a week so that we would not lose continuity in the incubation and nestling cycle, we rode out each storm, hoping for the best. Our tower creaked and swayed under the powerful winds. The nearby trees bent and scraped against the tower. Sudden gusts of wind tore at our canvas blind, threatening to rend it and expose us to the elements. We both were fearful for our safety, but fortunately our tower held firm, although we were a bit unnerved.

All kinglet nests we observed survived the storms and proved to be impervious to the elements. However, in 1955 our 53-foot tower did fail to withstand one storm after the nestlings had fledged. For 1½ months we had spent our daylight hours at the top of it. The day after our aerial observations were concluded, it toppled over.

There were other moments of excitement while we were quietly watching from our lofty perches. One morning while I was comfortably seated 60 feet from the ground, observing nestling activity in a tree on the bank of LaSalle Creek, I heard a sudden roar and saw a wall of water about 4 feet high rushing down the creek from the south. The beaver dam that was located just a couple of hundred yards away had burst, and 15 acres of water—which averaged about 7 feet in depth—were released directly toward my tree.

My first fear was that the rush of water would undermine the tree and topple it. Then it dawned on me that my car was parked next to the creek about 400 feet downstream in the path of the rushing water. I tried frantically to descend from the tree but the water at the base was too deep and flowing too swiftly.

It was about 15 minutes before I could safely leave the tree and survey the damage to my car. What a relief to see it still on the road. It was thoroughly bathed on the outside, but had leaked only a little.

Both the road and culvert just in front of my car were washed away. Since I was the only one aware of the break in the beaver dam and the flood that followed, I knew I'd be stranded on the wrong side of the creek until help arrived. Eventually the water passing over the break in the road subsided sufficiently so that I could drive across.

Nest lowering. Even though lowering had caused the loss of a kinglet nest, we decided to lower two more nests later in our study. Our second attempt involved a pair of kinglets that had chosen a double-headed black spruce crown for their second nest, 48 feet above the ground. Their

The cluster of twigs above the bucket is the crown of this tree that housed the nest. It was cut off just below the nest and lowered 10 feet. Its stem was put in a bucket of sand and water to prevent drying out of the needles.

first nest still housed nestlings, and the construction of their second nest, except for final work on the nest lining, had just been completed. About an hour after sunrise, I made a cut 9½ feet from the treetop and 2 feet below the nest and lowered the top 2 feet. The female did not visit her newly constructed nest during the three-hour observation period following the nest lowering.

The next day I checked her new nest and found one egg. I lowered the nest 2½ feet more, and began constructing a tree platform in a neighboring tree about 6 feet away and 38 feet above ground level. We chose that height because we felt the tree was sturdy enough at that point to support two people sitting in a blind.

In the 90 minutes that it took me to erect the tree platform, the adult kinglets did not visit the second nesting site. Both of them made feeding visits to their nestlings in the first nest. In late morning they flew to a tree next to my platform and engaged in coition twice within a quarter of an hour. The female did not return until midafternoon when she flew almost directly to the nest with lining material.

By the following day a second egg was in the nest. We lowered the nest 5½ feet, which was 10 feet below its original height of 48 feet, and within 1 foot of the end of our tree platform. The kinglets accepted the final lowering of their nest as if no change had taken place. No further nest lowering was necessary.

Our third attempt at nest lowering involved a nest that was 5 feet from the top of a balsam fir, 60.5 feet above ground. It contained nine eggs. We had been observing the birds from a tree platform in a white spruce, 54 feet above the ground and 12 feet from the nest. We thought the white spruce was sturdy enough at that level but not at 60 feet, so we cut the balsam fir 6 feet from the top, and lowered the nest segment 6 feet, the same level as our platform. This pair of kinglets also accepted the new site of their nest and allowed us to observe them during their nesting cycle.

View from the treetops of the spruce-tamarack bog on the northeast boundary of the park. This photo was taken from a kinglet nesting site 58 feet above the ground.

2

Study Locale

ALL OF THE KINGLET NESTS that we studied were located in Itasca State Park, which was established as a park in 1891 and named after Lake Itasca, the largest lake in the park. The headwaters of the Mississippi River are at the outlet of this lake. The park is located in northwestern Minnesota and is largely forest, part of which is virgin. The park covers 32,000 acres, including 3,000 acres of lakes and ponds and 1,500 acres of swamps. Of the 157 bodies of water within the boundaries of the park, 110 are large enough to be classified as lakes.

At the time of our study primary trees in the park's swamps and bogs were black spruce and tamarack, along with speckled alder, Bebb's willow, red osier dogwood, elm, and black ash (Marshall and Buell 1955). Quaking aspen, mixed with some birch and bur oak, dominated on 13,000 acres of the park; red pine on 5,700 acres; jack pine on 1,800 acres; spruce and balsam fir on 1,600 acres; and white pine on 800 acres (Hansen and Duncan 1954).

Mammals that were occasionally seen from our lofty perches in the spruce-tamarack bog in the northeast corner of the park were black bears, deer, coyotes, badgers, river otters, and porcupines. More prevalent were raccoons, eastern and least chipmunks, and red squirrels.

At Itasca, golden-crowned kinglets tend to prefer the

spruce-tamarack bogs for nesting sites. The first nest we studied, in 1954, was situated on the southeastern end of the campus where the caretaker lived and maintenance sheds were located. The area was improved and maintained throughout the birds' nesting cycle. The immediate kinglet area was bordered on all sides by a service road. The main road leading onto the forestry and biological station campus ran through the north end of the kinglet territory. Dominant trees were balsam fir, white spruce, red pine, northern white cedar, and tamarack, with a few scattered paper birch, quaking aspen, and jack pine. Most of the ground cover was periodically mowed.

In the four subsequent seasons of observing kinglets, 7 nests were located east of the main campus road in a black spruce-tamarack bog that was bordered by the main park highway on the west and by a gravel service road on the north. Ground cover included early low blueberry, Canada blueberry, downy arrowwood, juneberry, spreading dogbane, and bracken fern.

The remaining 11 nests were approximately 2 miles from the campus in the northeast boundary of the park in a black spruce-tamarack bog that was bordered by a gravel road on the north and by the main park highway to the west and southwest. Trees dominant in this area were black spruce and tamarack. Prevalent along the road were Bebb's willow, dwarf birch, red osier dogwood, and speckled alder. Dominant shrubs were American fly honeysuckle and wild sarsaparilla.

Associated birds. Nests located in or close to kinglet territories included those of the boreal chickadee; blue-gray gnatcatcher; rose-breasted grosbeak; chipping and white-throated sparrows; blackburnian, black-throated green, and golden-winged warblers; and common yellowthroat. Some of these birds competed with kinglets for food. Blackburnian warblers and kinglets had skirmishes on occasion.

Additional species seen or heard in kinglet territory were

the black-capped chickadee; brown-headed cowbird; brown creeper; American crow; black-billed cuckoo; alder, great crested, and least flycatchers; ruffed grouse; sharp-shinned hawk; blue and gray jays; red-breasted and white-breasted nuthatches; ovenbird; barred owl; northern parula; eastern phoebe; American robin; song sparrow; veery; red-eyed and solitary vireos; mourning, nashville, and pine warblers; eastern wood-pewee; and winter wren.

Climate. We found the climate of Itasca State Park during the May through August nesting season of the kinglet to vary widely. Although mean temperatures during this four-month period varied from 52° to 67°F (based on park records for 1940–56), lows were between 12° and 36°F and highs between 91° and 101°F! An average of 3 to 4 inches of precipitation fell during each of the four months, but extremes during 1940–56 ranged from 1 inch per month to 13 inches in July and 7 to 8 inches in each of the other three months.

In May of 1954, the year our study began, over 8 inches of snow fell, and even in July, a trace of snow was recorded. Occasionally we had frost in June and July in some areas of the park. And yet there were periods when the humidity and temperature were so high that we had to raise our blind for air circulation.

3

Vocalizations

GOLDEN-CROWNED KINGLET vocalizations are, for some people, very difficult to hear. In some unpublished notes that he supplied to A. C. Bent (1949), Francis H. Allen refers to the song of the kinglet as "a pleasing performance, beginning with a number of fine, high notes, and containing a lower-pitched and mellow willy, willy, willy that is quite charming." Bent describes a song of 9 notes in which the first 3 notes are the same as their winter notes, rather faint and lisping and uttered slowly; the second 3 are in a higher key, louder and fuller toned; the last notes are on a descending scale with increasing rapidity but decreasing volume, suggesting the last part of the chickadee's song.

"Vocalization," as used in this book, refers to all vocal sounds the bird produces. We recognized three major patterns, or types, of kinglet vocalization during our five seasons of study.

1. Call notes—These were either passive, consisting of one to 5 "tsee" notes on the same pitch, or active, consisting of the same "tsee" notes, but louder, more rapid, and strident.

2. Simple song—This was a series of up to 14 notes with the first 2 to 5 on the same pitch and the remainder ascending in less than halftone intervals. The simple song lasted up to two seconds.

3. Complex song—This started with the simple song for the first part and continued as a musical warble that dropped an octave or more in pitch for the second part; it lasted up to three seconds. Other variations of the complex song consisted of the same pattern but with the last part of the warble becoming chattery and harsh or much more melodious.

Passive call notes are used by the mating pair in communicating with one another, approaching the nest with food, alerting the nestlings of their presence when the young fail to gape for food, and locating and approaching the fledglings for feeding. They are also used by both sexes while the birds feed and during the long periods when the female is incubating eggs. During this time the male is perched in a nearby tree, generally preening and waiting for his mate's departure from the nest so that he can accompany her while she feeds. His call notes become active when she is foraging off the nest.

Active call notes are also used when either adult is alarmed or distressed. Kinglets use them in the presence of red squirrels, brown-headed cowbirds, blackburnian warblers, jays, sharp-shinned hawks, and occasionally chipping sparrows. The male uses these call notes when other kinglets invade his territory and when he proclaims his territory.

In addition to use during territorial defense, active call notes are frequently given by both sexes at other times. These are during nest construction (especially when the birds meet at the nest), during coition, and when the female refuses food brought to her by the male while she is incubating or when she refuses to get off the nest while brooding nestlings and he wants to feed the young. He usually taps her on the head when she does not cooperate, giving call notes. In the latter case, he seems to have a strong urge to feed, and she to brood.

The simple song is used in active defense. It is also used with call notes during stress or alarm. The song tends to be sharper, even strident, when a male is alarmed or in direct exchange with another male in a bordering territory. Occasionally the female uses the simple song to answer or call the male while she is on the nest or when she approaches the nest from a period off the nest.

Complex songs are primarily for proclaiming territory, but they are also used when red squirrels and jays are in the vicinity of the nest or near the fledglings. They are used frequently against blackburnian warblers and chipping sparrows. Both sexes use complex song while constructing their nests, especially when one bird is working materials into place and the other one is approaching the nest or waiting its turn to get on the nest with a load of nesting material. The complex song is often interspersed with the simple song.

Male kinglets vocalize in all types of situations. They vocalize while gathering nesting material, carrying it to the nest, and working it into place; before, during, and after coition; while approaching the nest with a bill stuffed with food to feed their mate or nestlings; upon leaving the nest; and while in flight. Vocalizing is done at all levels in the trees. It can be steady, one song after another, for several minutes or up to an hour or more, especially when alarmed by predators or neighboring kinglets. Generally, vocalization lasts several minutes or more, followed by intervals of silence.

Female kinglets occasionally call from the nest while incubating and brooding. Both sexes sing the melodious version of the complex song, but we heard this only while the kinglets were at the nest. The male sang it after feeding nestlings, and the female while incubating or brooding. We have been unable to link it to any specific behavior. It was done once by the female when she was incubating and a red squirrel chattered nearby. Ordinarily, however, female kinglets lay low in the nest when red squirrels are prowling nearby.

Female kinglets apparently do not assume any role in territorial defense when their mate is absent. Once when the male of a breeding pair disappeared during the nestling period, the female took over all the nesting duties except defending the territory through song. The vocalizing she did was primarily while approaching and leaving the nest at feeding times.

Kinglet vocalizing appears to be fairly intermittent

during the nestling period and after the young of the first nesting fledge. Later in the season, during the latter part of July and early August, less territorial vocalizing takes place, and the vocalizing that is done is primarily call notes for locating and feeding fledglings.

Rate of vocalization. The longest vocalizing sessions that we witnessed among the kinglets occurred in the presence of cowbirds and predators, especially red squirrels and jays. During such encounters, the most rapid vocalizing was composed of a series that consisted of one to three call notes. One male called 61 times in 3 minutes when a red squirrel was in a tree near the nest. Another red squirrel near the nesting site elicited a program lasting 32 minutes and numbering 458 vocalizations consisting primarily of simple and complex songs. Gray jays caused 139 vocalizations in 12 minutes from one male who stalked the jays, flitting from limb to limb as they moved about in the trees.

In another incident a male sang continuously when a red squirrel foraged in a tree near the fledglings. Most of the calls consisted of single strident "tsees." The female often joined her mate in the incident, and together they stalked the predator, maintaining a constant barrage of call notes.

One male kinglet became quite excited while his mate was incubating and a pair of blackburnian warblers was displaying and copulating toward the top of a nearby 50-foot aspen. In the 72 minutes preceeding the appearance of the warblers he had been perched in a fir tree 15 feet above the ground giving passive call notes. Upon arrival of the warblers he immediately interspersed call notes with song. He vocalized for 7 minutes and flew to the crown of another fir tree where he fed rapidly then continued flitting from one tree crown to another, cresting and constantly singing for 7 more minutes. He perched on dead limbs 15 to 20 feet from the ground where he preened, displayed his crown patch, and finally returned to the tops of different trees to feed again. He vocalized continuously until the blackburnian warblers left the area.

In addition to territorial singing it is common for the male to perch 25 to 50 feet from the nesting tree and between 15 and 40 feet above the ground, passively calling while the female incubates. In one such incident a male sang for a period of 72 minutes. However, when his mate left the nest to gather food, he changed his tune to active vocalizing and accompanied her at a lower level (15 to 40 feet) while she foraged in the crowns of the trees 60 to 70 feet above the ground. During the 28 minutes that she fed, he vocalized twice as much as he did during the time she was on the nest.

Much of the vocalizing done by the male during nest construction includes the complex song. During one of his 70-minute work periods, the male vocalized much more than his mate.

In comparing the amount of vocalizing done during different periods of one male's nesting cycle, we found that the least amount took place during the egg-laying period (22 songs per hour), while the most, during the incubation period (101 songs per hour). Vocalizations were counted from the blind near the nest between 7:00 A.M. and 12:00 noon.

One kinglet vocalized 22 times per hour during egg laying. Another vocalized 82 times; he had left an established territory and formed a new one, thus spending more time proclaiming his new area. More singing also took place during other nesting phases—incubation and nestling—when males were defending their territories from neighboring rivals. Territorial singing appears to be less frequent among pairs whose immediate borders are free from territorial rivals.

During egg laying there was less vocalizing. One male we watched did little singing after the fifth egg was laid and no singing during the following three days while eggs six, seven, and eight were being laid. He began vocalizing again after the ninth egg was laid. During the three days that the male was not heard, the female visited the nest to do work on its lining, but she did not vocalize either.

This same male almost lost his voice during five days of the nestling period. One day in June his voice started to become hoarse; the following day it was extremely squeaky and faint. It began improving two days later, and within four days was almost back to normal. Nonetheless, he continued to sing during this period at approximately the same rate as prior vocalizations.

A slight reduction in kinglet vocalizing was noted during rainy periods. However, during heavy downpours it was difficult to hear some of the vocalizations unless the birds were extremely close. I stood 12 feet below a male while he passively vocalized during a 15-minute downpour. He sang more often before it started to rain, so the rain had apparently dampened his spirit.

Singing and the time of day. Kinglets are not early vocalizers compared to many of the other local species. In mid-July of our second year the first kinglet vocalized at 4:44 A.M. In the meantime most other birds in the neighborhood had already made themselves known. It was still semi-dark (4:00 A.M.) when I had arrived at the blind, and the hermit thrush and common yellowthroat were already singing.

Kinglets tend to sing earlier after the eggs hatch and the care of nestlings begins. In mid-June after all eggs had hatched, one male began singing at 4:00 A.M., which was about 1½ hours before sunrise. He gave his last call at 8:10 P.M., ½ hour before sunset. By mid-July after the nestlings had fledged, he began singing at 4:37 A.M., quitting for the day at approximately the same time of evening as he had in June.

4

Territorial Behavior

MOST BIRDS ESTABLISH territories around their nests and defend them against species of their own kind. Males usually select the territories and must often defend them by fighting. Male kinglets had already established their territories and pair bonds when our studies began each season in mid-May. By that time kinglet pairs were already in the process of building nests or laying eggs.

Territory size. We determined the boundaries and dimensions of 11 territories by following the singing male and mapping his song perches. Lines connecting the outermost points of his wanderings were measured with a steel tape. These measurements were then plotted on a map, and the enclosed area was measured by dividing the areas into triangles and calculating their sizes. Territories ranged in size from 2.1 to 6.2 acres. They averaged 4.1 acres per territory.

Five territories were bordered on two sides by roads; three had roads on one side. In some cases a different type of plant community was on the opposite side of the road. On the northeast boundary of Itasca State Park the land sloped upward from the bog on the south and west sides of kinglet territories. Breeding kinglets did not venture there—probably because these areas had few coniferous trees.

Generally, the size of kinglet territories appears to be determined by the number of breeding kinglets competing for territories and the type of vegetation bordering their territories.

Responses to other kinglets. During nest building, egg laying, and incubation the male spends much time vocalizing from various perches throughout his territory. This territorial vocalizing is mostly done from dead branches of coniferous trees at 12 to 35 feet from the ground. The male is very attentive to the movements of his mate during incubation and brooding periods when she is off the nest. He remains perched on a limb in a neighboring tree, preening and intermittently vocalizing during much of the time that she is on the nest.

Whenever his mate leaves the nest, the male is quick to note her departure and gives a series of three to four rapid call notes. As she flits about, he increases his vocalizing while escorting her about the territory. When off the nest, she spends most of her time foraging in the crowns of the trees while he stays well below her, periodically displaying his crown patch.

After the eggs hatch, the male's attention is directed more toward feeding the young than escorting his mate. He makes himself conspicuous by vocalizing as he gathers food and carries it to the nest.

When a male kinglet invades the territory of his neighbor, the defender immediately flies to within a foot or two of the intruder, emits "tsee" notes in a rapid series of one to four, crests with the orange crown patch spread to the superciliary line, completely displacing the yellow, and bows his head toward his opponent. During this display he rapidly flaps his wings and flicks his tail. The intruder assumes the same aggressive posture as the defender. If neither one retreats, they may resort to physical contact.

We observed physical contact once in late June. The invading male had lost his mate and was taking care of six

47

fledglings. The defender was tending seven fledglings while his mate was incubating the eggs in her second nest. The intruder, before he actually breached the territory of his neighbor, had been singing vigorously from the tops of the trees along the border of the defender's territory, intermittently exposing his crown patch as though attempting to attract a new mate. The defender was singing less frequently and from a lower level as he gathered food for his fledglings. When the invader penetrated the territory and perched in a tamarack, the defender flew to within a foot of him. There they both postured and gave call notes in a series of one to four. Their crowns were fiery orange as they ascended, hopping from limb to limb in clockwise movement until they almost reached the top of the 30-foot tree. At that point they reversed directions and descended nearly to the ground.

Once again they reversed directions and ascended clockwise. When they were about 20 feet from the ground, the defender's mate joined the mock battle, positioning herself opposite her mate so that the invader was between them. For a moment all three birds were perched on the same branch in a straight line. The female bowed her head toward the invader, spread her yellow crown patch almost to its superciliary line, gave call notes in a series of one to four, flicked her tail, and flapped her wings rapidly. She remained with the 2 males for 2 minutes and then departed, leaving them to their quarrels. The defender's fledglings were approximately 40 feet away, perched in a black spruce, "tsipping" and preening.

After 22 minutes of posturing in the tamarack the two locked bills and tumbled 20 feet to the ground at my feet where they beat their wings rapidly for about 10 seconds. Suddenly, the invader broke loose and retreated to his own territory, pursued by the defender. After penetrating the intruder's territory about 75 yards, the defender returned to his own area. In this encounter the two kinglets defended and retained their own territories.

Another territorial invasion—in mid-June—resulted in the loss of one kinglet's territory. This happened when one male without a mate had his territory flanked by two others.

The first male's mate had disappeared two days earlier leaving a nest of nine cold eggs, five of them pipped and ready to hatch. The second male had seven nestlings, and the third one was caring for nestlings and had begun his second nest.

After his mate's disappearance the first male continued to defend his territory. He was doing much more singing than usual, mostly from the highest point of each of the trees in which he perched, displaying his orange crown patch repeatedly. On the third day after the disappearance of his mate his two male neighbors invaded his territory almost simultaneously while he was on one of his singing sprees. One invader landed about 20 feet above him and the other invader perched about 8 feet below him. The defender was perched in a black spruce about 25 feet from the ground.

The three birds carried on an intensive complex song battle while spreading their orange crown patches to the superciliary lines. The recently abandoned defender was the most excited of the three; he displayed by preening his breast rapidly. In approximately a minute the three males sang their complex song 42 times. Suddenly the defender flew off, disappeared over the treetops, and was not seen or heard in his territory by us again. During the next few days each of the two neighbors took over the part of the vanquished male's territory that bordered on his own.

In addition to this case of territorial expansion we observed one other change in territorial boundaries. One pair abandoned its established territory after two unsuccessful attempts at nesting and established a new territory about 200 hundred feet from the boundaries of its old one.

Territorial defense activity appears to cease with kinglets soon after their second brood fledges. One pair tolerated the invasion of two families of fledglings, which included the attending adults. One female, however, did not tolerate the intrusion of a male kinglet in her territory while she was caring for fledglings. She had been without a mate for four days, and when the male intruder landed on the same branch on which she was feeding her fledglings, she emitted three rapid call notes and flew at him. He immediately fled from her territory with her in close pursuit.

Defense against other species. Golden-crowned kinglets tolerate most other species of birds in their territory, but they may display aggressively to birds nesting or feeding close to their nests.

The chipping sparrow and blackburnian warbler also nest high in the crowns of black spruce, fir, and white spruce. Two chipping sparrow nests were found in black spruces in one kinglet's territory. One sparrow nest was 52 feet above the ground; the other was 54 feet. A blackburnian warbler also had a nest approximately 50 feet above the ground in a black spruce, 65 feet from the kinglet's nest. Frequent encounters were observed between all three species. These involved mutual calling and chasing, and occasionally posturing, tail flicking, and wing flapping.

On one occasion a male blackburnian warbler followed a male kinglet to his nest and perched a few inches above and behind the kinglet while he was about to feed the nestlings. The male kinglet emitted three strident call notes, fed the gaping nestlings, and then chased the intruder. On another occasion a blackburnian warbler clashed momentarily with a kinglet in midair, then chased it away. Both birds had nests within 40 feet of each other.

Kinglets occasionally attacked or displayed to black-capped and boreal chickadees. The clashes consisted of tail and wing flapping, accompanied by mutual calling, cresting, and chasing. Chickadees were chased by both male and female kinglets when they landed in the kinglet's nesting tree. A female kinglet would also occasionally become excited when blackburnian warblers, chipping sparrows, black-capped chickadees, or boreal chickadees vocalized in or near the nesting tree while she was incubating or brooding. She would crest, rise in the nest, emit soft "tsee" notes, or sometimes leave the nest to help her mate give chase.

Encounters with other less common species were also observed. On one occasion we watched a male kinglet and male black-throated green warbler engage in mutual calling and tail flipping. The two birds had nests approximately 75 yards apart.

On another occasion while a pair of kinglets was building

its third nest, a female brown-headed cowbird perched in a neighboring tree about 15 feet from the nest and watched them. The male kinglet dived at the cowbird and chased her, emitting rapid and strident call notes. A few days later while the female kinglet was incubating at the same nest she raised up and crested when a male cowbird called from a nearby tree.

The kinglet's nest is extremely small to accommodate a cowbird, but Friedmann (1971) reports that, in the files at the University of British Columbia, there are two records of the brown-headed cowbird parasitizing the golden-crowned kinglet. In one instance a fledged young cowbird was seen being fed by a pair of kinglets, and in the other, a young cowbird nearly ready to fly was observed on a kinglet nest.

Sometimes encounters with other birds involved the young kinglets as well as the adults. One time several kinglet fledglings were flushed from a limb of a red pine by a male common yellowthroat. They simply flew to another limb in the same tree, and the yellowthroat abandoned the chase. The male parent kinglet, however, flew to within 7 feet of the yellowthroat, emitted call notes in a series of three, crested, displayed his crown patch, and flipped his tail with each call note. The yellowthroat remained near the fledglings for about 20 seconds and then flew away. The male kinglet ate the insects that were in his bill and wiped his bill vigorously on a limb. However, on another occasion a black-billed cuckoo landed a few inches from the kinglet's seven fledglings, which were perched in a tight row in a red pine. The cuckoo looked them over for a few seconds and flew away. Neither of the kinglet parents was around at the time.

Frequent visits were made to kinglet nesting trees by great crested flycatchers, red-eyed vireos, and white-breasted and red-breasted nuthatches. These species were tolerated with no apparent reaction from the kinglets. We once watched a red-breasted nuthatch follow a female kinglet to her nest. While the kinglet fed her nestlings, the nuthatch looked on just inches away. The kinglet departed from her nest unperturbed, and the nuthatch remained at the nest's edge a few seconds longer before leaving.

Responses to predators. A bird that finds it necessary to lay nine eggs twice a year and raise two broods is one that is frequently preyed upon. The predator that stirred kinglets up more than any other was the red squirrel, which we saw or heard every day throughout the kinglet nesting cycle. Generally both parents became quite excited over the presence of red squirrels in their territory but paid little attention while these predators were on the ground or far away. Once the squirrels took to the trees nearby, however, the kinglets became attentive.

When squirrels approached to within 60 to 70 feet from the nest, kinglet parents would stalk them, keeping a distance of 1 to 4 feet from them, emitting strident call notes, partially cresting, spreading their crown patches, flicking their tails, and hopping about. Whenever a squirrel rushed a parent, the kinglet would fly up, momentarily hover just out of the squirrel's reach, and land nearby. On three different occasions we observed male kinglets diving and hitting red squirrels that had ventured to within 10 to 15 feet of the bird's nest.

When red squirrels chattered in the near vicinity and the female kinglet was on the nest incubating or brooding, she might cower or rise up, crest, emit soft "tsee" notes, preen rapidly, peck at nesting material, or leave the nest to stalk the squirrel, especially if her mate was already pursuing a squirrel. While one kinglet was incubating, a red squirrel chattered a few feet below the nest. The incubating female immediately cowered very low. The squirrel walked past the nest without seeing it (or the observer) and leaped to a neighboring tree. The female then rose in the nest, crested, and gave three soft "tsee" notes. As the squirrel departed, a badger crashed through the underbrush 40 feet below the nest. The female rose in the nest, peered over the edge, and once more gave three soft "tsee" notes.

Kinglets tend to show the same concern toward red squirrels after their nestlings fledge but are still under care. When a red squirrel approached to within 5 feet below seven perched fledglings that had been out of the nest two days, the male parent flew to about 1 foot from the squirrel, emitting strident call notes. The kinglet spread his crown patch, hovered out of reach when the squirrel rushed him, and continued to pursue the squirrel as it leaped from tree to tree in retreat. His mate joined him, and together they followed the rodent. In the meantime the fledglings remained quietly on their perch, huddled closely together. On two other occasions a male kinglet actually struck a red squirrel that was approaching fledglings on the same branch 5 to 6 feet away.

As mentioned in Chapter One, we felt obliged to kill red squirrels during the study in order to protect our nests. Most of them found the nest or were about to locate it, and we were not about to abort our study after a tower or tree platform was constructed. We also felt that the squirrels found the nest because we left a trail for them.

Territorial defenses were also observed against several avian predators. While on a feeding visit to his nest, one male kinglet heard the call of a blue jay that was partially hidden in the foliage of a tree about 40 feet away. The kinglet quickly swallowed his load of insects, wiped his bill vigorously on a limb, and hopped about among the branches in various trees between his nest and the jay, emitting single call notes. At times the kinglet would expose himself fully on a limb with his crown patch partially spread, and at other times he would be partly or completely hidden among the twigs. Throughout his ordeal, the kinglet vocalized constantly and collected insects until his bill was so stuffed it was barely recognizable. The vocalizing was composed mostly of call notes in a series of three but also included four complex songs. He did not return to feed the nestlings for the duration of our observation period, which terminated 74 minutes after the jay left the area.

On several occasions during the incubation and brooding periods of female kinglets the distant calls of blue jays elicited a mild reaction. However, when the jays called in the immediate nesting area, the female kinglets reacted by cowering or rising in the nest, emitting soft call notes, and on a few occasions leaving the nest.

We frequently saw a pair of sharp-shinned hawks in the territories of three breeding pairs of kinglets. On one occasion a sharpshin landed about 30 feet from one of the kinglets' nests. The male kinglet hopped about in the surrounding trees and gave strident call notes for 9 minutes. Each call consisted of a series of one to three "tsee" notes. Apparently the kinglet was trying to attract the attention of the hawk toward himself and away from the nest.

5

The Nest

W E WERE VERY FORTUNATE to study a bird species that tolerated our close proximity and allowed us to observe their nest-building activities from only a few feet away. We did not learn if the male, female, or both select the nest site. The kinglets we studied nested either in the crowns of tall black spruce or balsam firs or on the underside of radiating white spruce branches. Since the birds also frequented these same places when they fed or the male proclaimed his territory, it was impossible to know when they were at the nest until it had been erected. Once they disappeared into the foliage, their activities became secret.

Nest construction. Both sexes share in nest building, but the female plays the leading role in both collecting and placing materials. The nest is rather complicated, and a great deal of work and skill goes into its construction. We carefully watched the construction of two complete nests plus one that was deserted when nearly completed. The construction of three other nests was observed cursorily.

A characteristic pattern is followed to begin nest building. The first materials are attached to corner twigs, and the nest takes on the shape of a square with hammocklike strands connecting all four corners. These strands are made up mostly of spider's web, silky bristles of cotton grass, and fine stringy brown- and buff-colored material resembling bark shreds. Several loads of this type of material may be brought to the nest site before being worked into place.

The female secures a strand to one twig and stretches the free end to the opposite twig where she fastens it on the inside. She does this by approaching the twig from the outside and twisting her head around to the inside. If the material does not stretch easily, she takes it in her bill and flutters over to the desired point. If that fails, she attaches the free end to the point where it stops stretching. However, some strands are so flexible that they stretch from one corner twig to another one and then part of the way back.

After a layer of this stretchable material is worked into place, moss is tucked into the stringy runners. These two procedures are alternated until the base is completed. Then work begins on the walls. The nest cup is shaped by the female rolling from side to side and kicking her feet while making quarter, half, and even full turns. Usually, three or four twigs are incorporated into the outer nest walls for support.

On occasion the female appeared hesitant about where to put nesting material brought in by herself or her mate. After attaching material to one twig, she would pull it loose, attach it to a different one, pull it free again, and tuck it into a different part of the nest.

After the layer of moss has been added, lichens are usually brought in and randomly attached on the outside. Strips of paper birch bark or other similar materials are used for part of the inside walls and lining. Kinglets collected lichen from black spruce branches, bark from balsam fir and paper birch, and dead black spruce needles from the ground. In our observations, all of this material was collected from within 50 feet of the nest tree.

Sometimes bringing in nesting material required considerable persistence and/or effort. A female, observed gathering moss at the base of an alder, took hold of a piece in her bill and pulled back, fluttering like a hummingbird in midair.

The moss broke loose, and she fell the few inches to the ground, recovered, took another hold on it, and repeated the procedure until she again fell to the ground. Each time she retained the piece of moss that broke off. She braced her feet against the trunk, again tugged at the moss and fluttered in midair, only to fall to the ground when the moss came loose. She continued this until her bill was stuffed with moss and then flew to her partially completed nest.

In addition to watching how nests were built, we were able to see other kinglet behavior during nest construction. We spent 18 hours observing one pair build its nest, one of us in the tower, the other on the ground. During that period the male made 42 trips and the female made 179 trips to the nest with building materials. The male visited the nest alone on nine occasions with no nesting material, and the female, four times. The male uttered passive call notes at the nest on 33 of his visits with materials and continued calling while working at the nest on 14 of these visits. On two occasions when the male arrived with nesting materials, the female was putting her load in place, and he hopped about impatiently, emitting a series of rapid call notes. When she finally finished her work, she removed the material from his bill and put it in the nest.

Twice the male came with his bill full of insects and gave a series of call notes as he shook the partially completed nest with his feet. He finally swallowed the food and left. We observed him feeding his mate on three occasions during nest construction.

The female also called while she approached the nest with material. She continued calling while working on the nest on all visits except one. The male accompanied her on the vast majority of her visits to the nest. He preceded her nine times and stood calling on the nest until she arrived. He then flew off and continued calling from a neighboring tree while she worked.

Coition took place on the nest four times during its construction. This was observed on the first day of nest construction after a hammock of fibers had been stretched between two twigs. The female called the male by flattening out

This pendulum-type kinglet nest was built in a white spruce. More typical kinglet nests were constructed with twigs for basal support.

on the hammock while fluttering her wings and twittering. He mounted her for about five seconds and then flew off. On the fourth day of nest construction, after the female came in with some lining material, she gave four call notes followed by a chorus of the full song. Her mate sang five rounds of the complex song in rapid succession, then mounted her. After about seven seconds he flew off; she hopped onto the limb supporting the nest, flattened out again, and called. The male reappeared and again coition followed. Afterward the female hopped back on the nest and began shaping it with her body. The male returned within a minute and mounted her for a third time.

Coition by other pairs at or near the nest was also observed but during the period of egg laying. One pair was seen copulating on a limb near their nest three days after the last egg was laid. The female instigated it by calling, twittering, and then flattening out on the limb.

During the third nesting attempt of the nest-building pair, the female made 323 trips with material; the male, only 12. He spent much of his time establishing and defending his territory.

We watched the pair at this nest for 38 hours, beginning when the first small fiber hammock had just been stretched between two twigs. Four days later the nest was virtually completed. On the sixth day after beginning nest construction, the first egg was laid. However, the female continued to bring in nest lining. Throughout egg laying she made nest improvements, primarily on the nest lining. She pulled feathers from one place and poked them into another place and carted away spruce needles and down. The nest this pair built hung as a pendulum and was essentially supported by surrounding twigs.

Nest dimensions. Kinglet nests are cup-shaped and deep, with the inside rims slightly arched inward. The nest cavity is almost circular. The cup stretches considerably before the nestlings fledge. For five nests we observed, the outside diameter increased nearly an inch from before egg hatching to after fledging (Table 5.1).

Table 5.1. Mean dimensions for five nests shortly before eggs hatched and after nestlings fledged

Nest dimension	Centimeters		Inches	
	Before	After	Before	After
Inside diameter	4.1	5.5	1.61	2.16
Outside diameter	7.5	9.7	2.95	3.81
Inside depth	4.0	3.2	1.57	1.25
Outside depth	7.7	5.1	3.03	2.00
Wall thickness	2.0	1.3	0.78	0.51

Source: Galati and Galati 1985.

Nest materials. Nineteen nests were collected and analyzed for nest materials. Most of them contained lichens scattered throughout the inner and outer walls and bottom. The interior bottoms of the nests were lined with fine strips of paper birch bark, moss, lichen, deer hair, and bird feathers. The outer walls consisted chiefly of mosses, strands of spider's web, cotton grass, parts of insect cocoons, and some unidentifiable brown-colored, stringy, stretchable material.

Minot (1877) was the first ornithologist to describe the nest of a golden-crowned kinglet. In a forest of evergreens and white birches in the White Mountains of New Hampshire, the nest hung 4 feet above the ground from a spreading hemlock bough. It was globular, with an entrance in the upper part, and was composed of hanging moss, ornamented with bits of dead leaves, and lined chiefly with feathers. It contained six young birds.

Brewster (1888) found three kinglet nests in tall, slender spruces near Winchendon, Massachusetts. One was about 60 feet above the ground and 2 feet from the treetop; the second was approximately 50 feet above the ground and 20 feet below the top of the tree; and the third was 30 feet above the ground.

> Outwardly they were composed chiefly of green mosses . . . prettily diversifed with grayish lichens . . . ,the general tone of the coloring, however, match [sic] closely that of the surrounding spruce foliage. The interior at the bottom was lined with exceedingly delicate strips of soft inner bark and fine black rootlets similar to, if not identical with, those which almost invariably form the lining of the nest of the Black-and-yellow Warbler [now known as the magnolia warbler]. Near the top were numerous feathers of the Ruffed Grouse, Hermit Thrush, and Oven-bird, arranged with the points of the quills down, the tips rising to, or slightly above, the rim and arching inward over the cavity, forming a screen that partially concealed the eggs (Brewster 1888).

Nest heights. Roberts (1936) reported the approximate heights of three kinglet nests in Minnesota as 35 to 40 feet from the ground. These nests were in spruce trees growing in typical sphagnum bogs. Swedenborg (1939) also reported a nest with five young near the top of a 30-foot spruce.

The kinglets in our study area generally preferred to nest in the crowns of trees. The average height of 19 nests that we found in Itasca State Park was 50.3 feet. All nests in black spruce and balsam fir were in the upper tree crowns just a few inches from the trunk. All but one of these nests not only rested on radiating twigs but also were supported by branches that had been incorporated into the walls near the nest rim. The lone exception had no basal support; it was supported by twigs on the rim. The four nests in white spruce were between 6 and 13 feet from the trunk, were suspended by the rims on radiating twigs, and had no basal support.

If kinglets displayed a preference toward a compass point when building their nests, it was to the east or southeast (11 nests were on the east; 6, on the southeast; 1 on the southwest; and 1 on the northwest). Prevailing winds at Itasca are westerly. All the east and southeast nests on the leeward side were high in the tree crowns, between 3 and 5 feet from the treetop. The nest on the exposed northwest side was the lowest one (27 feet), but it was only 15 feet east of a planted windbreak of tall balsam fir.

All nests were so well concealed that they weathered all wind and rainstorms and were never reached by the sun's rays. By being a few inches from the trunk in the black spruce and balsam fir, nests escaped any rain that might trickle down the trunk. The foliage was generally so dense around the nests that they could not be seen from above or from nest level. We always had to part some of the twigs to observe nest activity. The four nests in white spruce trees were on the underside of long branches near the tips. They, too, were completely hidden from view from the top or at nest level but could be partially seen from below.

Dates of nest building. Kinglets in northern Minnesota tend to nest later than those in northeastern states and provinces, perhaps because spring arrives much later in Minnesota. Bent (1949) quotes Robie Tufts, who reported finding two nests just started in Nova Scotia on April 10. Bent also mentions that Cordelia J. Stanwood informed him she found a half-finished nest near Ellsworth, Maine, on April 25.

The earliest nest building that we observed in Minnesota was on May 18. We watched that pair through two nesting cycles. The first egg was laid on May 24; the fledglings became independent July 20 (62 days from the beginning of nest construction). Their second nest was begun on June 24; these fledglings gained independence on August 21 (58 days from the time the nest was started). The span of time covering both nests was 94 days.

Golden-crowned kinglets generally seem to begin their second nest before the nestlings fledge from the first nest. When one nest we were watching was raided by a predator, the kinglets began building their second nest the following morning. They deserted the second nest after they had been working on it for three days, probably because of our activity near the nest (I was busily building a tree platform next to the branch that housed their nest). The following morning they were seen constructing their third nest.

On two other occasions, pairs whose first nests were destroyed by predators or abandoned also started nest construction the following day. One pair deserted its second nest after four days and began a third one less than 24 hours later. Generally birds are more apt to desert nests near the beginning of the nesting cycle, but their attachment to the nest becomes stronger as the cycle progresses, and their tolerance toward intrusions increases.

6

Eggs

BIRDS LAY DIFFERENT NUMBERS of eggs. Some lay only 1 while a few lay as many as 20. Generally 4 to 8 are laid. Eggs may be white, colored, or spotted. Colored eggs blend with the surroundings for protection.

Roberts (1936) describes the golden-crowned kinglet's eggs as white to dull cream, speckled with pale brown and faint lilac. Brewster (1888) describes kinglet eggs as being mostly ovate, with some being elliptical-ovate and some elliptical-oval. We found that brown markings, varying from tiny dots to large blotches, were distributed over the entire shell, especially around the larger ends. Those eggs with the lightest ground color were most heavily blotched at the larger ends, and the rest of the shell was sparsely marked. The whitest, most sparsely spotted eggs were the freshest, showing that they were the last ones laid.

I took measurements on one clutch of eggs that was about ready to hatch when the female disappeared. These nine eggs averaged 13 millimeters long by 10 millimeters wide.

Six eggs in another nest were weighed shortly after the sixth egg was laid. Five of the eggs were again weighed 14 days later, just about the time they were expected to hatch. All eggs lost weight during incubation, presumably through evaporation of moisture through the shell. In this clutch all but one egg hatched. This latter egg was apparently infertile because by the end of incubation, its weight had dropped 42 percent. Average weight loss of those eggs that hatched was just under 10 percent.

Eggs in a second nest were also weighed the day before they hatched. The average weight of all the eggs in this clutch was 0.6 grams (compared to an average weight of 0.7 for the four eggs that hatched in the other nest). Of the nine eggs in the second nest, one failed to hatch, and two nestlings died in the nest on the third day after hatching. Unfortunately, a predator robbed the nest on the fourth day after hatching, which ended our information gathering for that clutch.

Egg numbers and clutch initiation. In 13 nests under observation 8 had nine eggs for the first clutch, 3 nests had eight eggs in the second clutch, 1 nest was raided by a predator after the seventh egg was laid, and 1 nest was deserted after seven eggs were laid.

For the 13 nests we were watching when eggs were laid, the earliest a first clutch was begun was May 12 and the latest was May 27. The earliest date for the start of the second clutch (among those kinglets that were successful with their first clutch) was June 22 and the latest date, July 1. Within the same year the spread of days for the earliest egg-starting dates ranged from 7 to 15.

For several other nests we were able to calculate when clutches were started. A nest found on June 24 already had nine eggs, which began hatching July 3. Since incubation takes approximately 15 days, the clutch was probably started around June 10. Spring was behind its normal period by two weeks that year.

Two nests contained nine nestlings when they were found. Young in the first nest fledged June 16. Assuming 8 days for eggs to be laid (not counting the day the first egg was laid), 18 days the average time for nestlings to be in the nest, and 15 days the average time of incubation, that clutch must

This nest contained nine eggs that were laid on consecutive days.

have been started May 6. The nestlings in the second nest fledged July 20, so this was undoubtedly a second nest. Using the same yardstick for calculation, that clutch was probably started around June 9. Spring came a little earlier to Itasca that year.

Time of egg laying. Kinglets apparently lay their eggs early in the morning on successive days until the clutch is complete. We checked one nest at midnight on two consecutive nights. No additional eggs were in the nest at that hour, but in each case there was another egg in the nest at 4:00 A.M. the following morning.

The only time we knew almost precisely when an egg was laid was in mid-June. After making several trips with nesting material, the female arrived at 8:15 A.M. with a large feather. She tucked it into the side of the nest, made a half circle in four motions, stuck her head into the side of the nest, turned in a half circle to the right in three movements, rolled from side to side, and then sank low in the nest. After remaining in the nest for six minutes, she departed, leaving her first egg.

One night at midnight after we had checked a kinglet nest to see if the female had started laying her eggs, we were treated to an unusual sideshow in the middle of the road. Our headlights caught some activity about 300 feet ahead. We slowed down to within 25 feet of whatever it was. Directly in front of us were three young raccoons with an adult, and about 10 feet beyond them were three young skunks with one adult. Oblivious to us and our bright headlights, they were playing some sort of game. The three little skunks would rush up to the raccoons in a sidling manner and then run full speed back to their parent. The infant raccoons would return the honors and then scoot back to their parent. This continued at least a half dozen times until suddenly the youngsters stopped their game and scurried off the road and into the underbrush. I switched to my high beams and noticed three intruders—a female black bear with two small cubs. So ended the circus performance on the road. We didn't learn anything about kinglet eggs that night, but trying had been worth it!

7

Incubation

FEMALE BIRDS USUALLY INCUBATE the eggs. However, there are some species where both sexes share in this duty and others where only the male bird incubates. Incubation among kinglets is performed by the female only. During a 10-minute period that the female was away from her nest one cold morning, egg surface temperature dropped from 104° to 86°F. When she returned she was able to heat the eggs up to 100°F in only 35 seconds and to 102°F by the end of 15 minutes. After measuring temperatures of various clutches of eggs, we found that the heat applied to the eggs ranged from 102° to 105°F. (In Chapter One we described methods used to take egg temperatures.)

Length of incubation. Incubation usually began in small steps toward the end of egg laying. One female did not begin spending time at her first nest until the last of her nine-egg clutch was laid. At her second nest she began spending time on the nest after her seventh of eight eggs was laid. Once incubation began at both nests, the female spent an average of 71–82 percent of her time each day at the nest. The average length of time per attentive period at these nests was 31–34 minutes. The average length of time she was inat-

*Only the female kinglet incubates. The nest was
completely hidden from view.*

tentive or away from the nests was 6–7 minutes. The range was 4 to 38 minutes.

Another female began attentiveness (14 percent of the time on the nest over an eight-hour period) after the second egg was laid, but she apparently did not apply enough heat for incubation. She did begin spending over half of her time on the nest after the seventh egg was laid. From that day to the day the last egg hatched she spent 73 percent of her time on the eggs. Attentiveness for this female ranged from 1 to 17 minutes. Her inattentiveness was from 6 to 240 minutes.

Nice (1954) has proposed that the time from laying of the last egg to the hatching of the last young is generally a satisfactory indicator of the incubation period; Nice's formula proved to be accurate with the kinglets. In the above case, incubation for that clutch of eggs was 15 days. In observations made of another female no attentiveness was observed during either nesting cycle until the last egg was deposited. Using Nice's formula, the incubation time at both nests was 15 days. Actual hatching dates are given in Galati and Galati (1985).

Incubation behavior. The female kinglet is fidgety during incubation. Generally, she is very attentive to sounds in the immediate environment, and her normal routine is a restless one. She changes directions every few seconds by turning from quarter to full turns or more; rising and resettling; pecking at nesting material; yawning; imitating drinking motions; and preening her breast, belly, primary and secondary feathers, and tail. She occasionally hops onto the rim of the nest and peers inside then hops back in.

However, females may remain quiet for several minutes and even doze off to sleep with their eyes closed. One female left her incubation duties momentarily, flew into the blind, and landed on my notebook. She pecked at my pencil while I was taking notes, then flew back to the nest and continued incubating. Later that day when Carlyn stroked the bird's wing and back, the kinglet closed her eyes and appeared to go to sleep.

Another time the female poked her bill into the nest bottom and remained motionless, apparently asleep. After 10 minutes Carlyn became concerned and shook the nest. There was no response even when the bird was poked. However, when Carlyn picked up the bird, its eyes slowly opened and blinked twice. When returned to the nest, the kinglet promptly closed her eyes and apparently dozed off again. It was a warm day with little wind.

Carlyn and I had the feeling that adult kinglets came to accept us and were not concerned with our activities in the blind. When we had visitors, the birds flew to the blind zipper or landed on us, looked over our human guests, but only alighted on the most frequent of our visitors.

The male quite often visits the nest to feed his mate during the incubation stage. The male of one pair we watched fed his mate 49 times in 75 hours of observation over a period of 15 days while she incubated. Observations were then being conducted at this nest from 7:00 A.M. to 12:00 A.M. each day. However, during their second nesting he fed her only 7 times in the same amount of observation over the same length of incubation. During this period he was busily feeding the fledglings from the first nest. His mate seldom made feeding visits to them.

The largest number of visits in a 5-hour observation period made by the male to feed his mate while she incubated was 14 made on the seventh day after incubation at the first nest had started. This male made no feeding visits from the ninth through the thirteenth day of incubation. The male always called as he approached the nest with food for his mate. She rose in anticipation, crested, gaped, and fluttered her wings. During one visit the male fed her an insect larva. She returned it to him, and then took it back. He retrieved it from her, and once again she removed it from his bill, this time eating the larva.

There is much exchange of call notes between the female on the nest and the male roaming through his territory. During one exchange the male called 56 times, giving three to eight call notes each time. She responded 54 times, using one to seven call notes each time.

Males frequently accompany their mates to the nest when they return from a period off the nest, and they also join them quite often when the females leave the nest. In nearly all cases the females approached the nest by first landing several feet below the nest and then hopping from limb to limb in a spiral pattern until the nest was reached. The males also approached from below the nest but generally pursued a more direct path.

During the first nesting of one pair the female came in with a load of insects as though to feed her eggs on the twelfth day of incubation. (She repeated this behavior on the eighth, twelfth, and thirteenth days during incubation of the second nest.) She addressed her eggs, shaking the nest by alternately stamping her feet on the rim of the nest. She gave rapid call notes before she finally ate the food. This was also the general procedure used when feeding nestlings that did not respond to her.

This same type of behavior was observed with another pair. The female came to the nest with food and tried to feed eggs once after the fifth egg was laid, and three times during incubation. The male also attempted to feed eggs on three occasions. His first attempt was during the first day of incubation. In two other instances while his mate was incubating, the male arrived at the nest with food and the female failed to respond. He stamped vigorously on the nest edge, gave rapid call notes, and tried to force the food on her. She refused the food and left the nest. He remained and continued to shake the nest and give call notes. Finally, he ate the food and left the nest. On his second visit he was successful in forcing her to take food after she had initially refused it. However, she hopped on the edge of the nest and tried to get the eggs to respond to feeding. She finally ate the food herself and then resettled on the nest. Perhaps this type of behavior was all part of courtship feeding.

The male kinglet is about to feed nine hungry nestlings. Both parents share in feeding duties.

8

Nestlings

BECAUSE KINGLETS TOLERATED our presence at the very edge of their nests, we occasionally observed the exact moment when a nestling emerged from its shell. The earliest date we recorded for eggs hatching during the first nesting cycle was June 4, when seven of nine eggs hatched. The latest date for the first clutch to hatch was July 6, when the last of nine eggs hatched.

Eggs may hatch at any time during the day or night. Seven eggs in one nest hatched during the day, beginning at 8:05 A.M. and ending at 3:29 P.M. In another nest all the eggs hatched during the night and before 7:00 A.M. on two consecutive days. Hatching may also span both daylight and nighttime hours. In one nest three eggs hatched during the night, two in early afternoon, and two more the following morning. Three clutches took two days to hatch, two hatched over a period of three days, and two required four days.

Eggshells are either eaten or removed by both parents. In one instance the female carried an eggshell to a neighboring tree where she ate it. Unhatched eggs are not removed from the nest as far as we know. Eggs disappeared, but whether they hatched and the nestlings died and were then removed is not known.

For the first three to five days after the last egg hatches, almost as much time is spent brooding the young (covering the young with wings to keep them warm or cool, whatever the situation requires) as was spent incubating the eggs. Brooding time diminishes until between the sixth and ninth day when it stops, possibly because the nestlings will no longer tolerate it. All the females under observation tried brooding longer, but the young became so active that the females did not have a moment's peace.

Active nest stretching takes place throughout the incubation and nestling periods and is apparently done entirely by the female. She pokes her bill and head into the sides of the nest and pushes forward, while at the same time, pushing to the rear side with her feet. She also pokes her bill into the nest bottom, then rolls from side to side. She has a difficult time nest stretching when the nestlings no longer wish to be brooded. Nonetheless, she attempts it while they toss her about, poking their heads between her legs, wings, and tail feathers. The nestlings also cause the nest to stretch as they gain weight and become more active.

One pair had their nest stretched beyond its limits, probably because this nest did not contain lining, and the walls were loosely constructed. A hole, large enough for nestlings to fall through, originated in the bottom of the nest. The nest was located 57 feet from the ground, hanging like a pendulum from the underside of a black spruce branch. It was the only nest found in either black spruce or balsam fir that had no basal support.

One morning I found a nestling hanging by its head from the bottom of this nest. Another was a few feet below the nest, balancing on the end of a twig; a third was on the ground in some moss. All were still alive, so I returned them to the nest after making a hammock out of my handkerchief and tying the loose ends around the branch above the nest. The weight of the nest and its occupants rested firmly in the hammock. Fearing that my white handkerchief would attract predators, I replaced it later the same day with half of a gray plastic toilet float. I had drilled numerous air holes into the bottom and sides of the float and attached two pieces of wire to the upper rim. At the nest tree I wound the wires around the branch above the nest so that they supported the weight of the float, nest, and nestlings. All nine nestlings successfully fledged five days later.

Feeding of nestlings. Although both parents feed nestlings, the male does a greater share during the early part of the first nesting cycle when the female is spending most of her time brooding. However, when the nestlings are no longer brooded, the feeding visits tend to equalize. The female again falls behind when she starts building her second nest. The male sometimes interrupts his feeding visits if predators are near or if his territory needs defending from other kinglets.

Generally, the male carries more food per feeding visit than does the female. Food items are usually tiny during the early nestling stage and increase in size and number as the young grow larger. One male tried feeding inappropriately large items to his newly hatched young. He was unsuccessful, and the insects kept falling into the nest. Meanwhile, the female continued bringing small items and had no feeding problems. On numerous feeding visits she approached the nest while her mate was attempting unsuccessfully to feed larger items. She broke tiny bits from the food in his bill and fed the nestlings. He apparently learned and, before the day was over, brought tiny items.

Because males bring more food, they are able to feed more nestlings per hour. We concluded this after observing four pairs during their complete nestling periods of 16–19 days. Feeding visits were counted during a 5-hour period that ended at noon. Males fed three to seven nestlings per hour during this period, while females fed two to four.

Just after the young kinglets hatch they seldom respond when adults arrive with food. The adults then shake the nest by stamping their feet rapidly on the nest's rim and give call notes in a series of three to four until they get a response. On one occasion when we were watching newly hatched young on their first day, they responded to their parents' feeding arrival only 3 times in 18 trips. When the nestlings were 2 days old, they increased their response to 18 times in 26 feeding visits. However, when 3 days old, they responded only 7 times in 23 visits. At 4 days they responded 10 times in 14 visits. The approach or presence of the parents did not invariably bring a reaction until the oldest nestlings in the brood were 6 days old.

Nestlings in another brood, although generally accepting food as it was brought, didn't respond on 3 visits during the first 3 days after hatching. On these occasions the parent swallowed the food and left. Such lack of response by young nestlings may be the result of overfeeding.

Both adults appear to be impatient when nestlings do not swallow food quickly. This happens quite often when the food items are large. In one nest an adult moth was placed in five different mouths before a nestling successfully swallowed it.

Not all food items brought to the nestlings were eaten. Many spiders were partially swallowed, then regurgitated by the young. Sometimes when this occurred, the parents tried to feed the spiders to other nestlings, which also rejected them.

The largest number of feeding visits made by a female during a 5-hour period was 129 when the oldest nestlings were 14 days. She was taking care of the young by herself. The smallest number was 0 while the female was building a second nest.

The largest number of feeding visits by a male in 5 hours was 43 when the oldest nestling was 6 days; the smallest number of visits was 3, by the same male on the first day that the eggs began to hatch.

The mean number of feeding visits by both parents gradually increases from the first day the eggs hatch until the nestlings are between 7 and 8 days old. Then the number of visits levels off, with minor fluctuations.

However, there was one exception when the female of one pair dramatically increased her feeding visits after her mate was no longer around to help. These visits took place over 16- to 17-hour observation periods beginning at 4:00 A.M. when the nine nestlings were 11 and 14 days old. When the female had to feed the nestlings alone, the number of feeding visits she made per hour (19) almost tripled the number she made while her mate was still helping (7). But she brought less food per trip because the total number of feedings only doubled (568 versus 282).

In addition to the number of parents available to bring food, the number of young in the nest also affects how many feeding visits kinglets make. During a series of 5-hour observation periods ending at noon, two pairs with nine nestlings each made respectively an average of 14 and 9 feeding trips per hour to the nest. Two other pairs with seven and six nestlings each made an average of only 8 feeding visits per hour to the nest.

One other factor that affects feeding trips by parents is the start of a second nest. Two pairs we were watching began a second nest on the eighth day after their eggs began to hatch in the first nest. Each female laid her first egg in the second nest on the fourteenth day after the first egg had hatched in the first nest. Both pairs completed second nests in five days. In each case the first egg was laid in the second nest on the sixth day from the start of nest construction. In both cases the males of both pairs did very little work on the second nest.

The female with seven nestlings began reducing her feeding visits the day before she began her second nest, and she continued this trend until the fourth day of nest construction. She made only 1 visit on the third day of construction, and none on the fourth. Then she resumed her normal number of feeding visits, which averaged 16, on the day her first egg was laid.

However, the female with nine young did not reduce her feeding visits until the third day after beginning second nest construction, when she made only 4 visits. She made the greatest number of feeding visits to her nestlings on the first and fourth days of nest construction (26 and 28, respectively; her average number per day had been 17). She made only 2 the day her first egg was laid in the second nest.

After starting their second nests, both females left most of the feeding duties to their mates. This is shown in the percentage of nestlings fed. For the pair with seven young the male fed 73 percent of all the nestlings and the female, only 27 percent during the nesting cycle. In this pair's second nest each parent fed 50 percent of the nestlings. For the pair with nine young the male fed 64 percent of all the nestlings and the female, 36 percent. Unfortunately, the second nesting of this pair was unsuccessful, so no further comparisons were possible.

Conflicts in behavior between nest building and feeding. After one female kinglet began construction on her second nest, she showed what appeared to be ambiguous behavior between working on her new nest and feeding the young in the old nest. This was first observed on the fifth day of construction when she was lining the new nest. Carlyn was watching nest construction, and I was observing the nest with the young. Since the nests were only 200 feet apart, we were able to shout back and forth to communicate. We didn't have to yell too loudly to be heard either.

Having made no feeding visits to the nestlings the previous day, the female kinglet approached the nestlings with lining material, which included deer hair, and fed it to two gaping mouths. She returned later with more lining items and fed one of the four gaping mouths. She then brought a large load of fine moss and fed all of it to one nestling. During the five hours we watched her, she made only 4 feeding visits, 3 of them with nest-lining materials and only 1 with insect food.

The following day, after laying the first egg in her new nest, she made 16 feeding visits to the nestlings; 4 were with nest-construction items. On her first visit with nest materials she fed one young a down feather; I removed part of it. She returned with insects, fed one young, lingered momentarily, pulled a feather out of the side of the nest, flew off, returned in two minutes with the same feather, and fed it to a nestling. The youngster would not swallow the feather, so the female removed it, fed it to another gaping mouth, and departed. I also removed that feather.

She returned shortly with some stringy material and fed one nestling, picked up some loose deer hair on the same branch as the nest and fed another, and pulled a feather out of the nest interior and fed it to a third young. Since the nestlings did not immediately swallow that type of food, I removed all traces. Within minutes the female returned with lichen and other lining items and fed another nestling, who promptly spit it out.

This ambiguous behavior continued on the seventh, eighth, and ninth days after the start of the second nest. By this time construction of this nest was complete, and it contained two eggs. On 4 occasions the female arrived at the first nest with deer hair, feathers, down, and/or other nest-lining materials that she fed to the gaping mouths in the nest. Three times, the nestlings swallowed what was stuffed in their mouths; only one promptly spit it out.

On 8 other occasions the female went to the first nest and began pulling out lining materials—deer hair, feathers, down, and moss—from within it. Some material, such as loose hair, she just scooped up from the nest cup. Other materials, such as feathers, had been woven into the nest and had to be jerked out, once causing a break in the nest wall. Four times the female picked up these nest materials and flew to the second nest without giving them to the nestlings. The other 4 times she fed the nesting materials to her gaping nestlings, which generally swallowed this food. Only once did two nestlings refuse some deer hair the female tried to feed them.

In addition to mistaking nesting materials for food, this same female seemed to mistake food for nesting materials! Once after nest construction was complete except for the lining, the female arrived at the second nest with a load of insects and incorporated them into the nest wall. On the following day she arrived with another billful of insects and again worked them into the nest wall.

Three weeks later when the nestlings in her second nest were 5 and 6 days old, she pulled a loose feather from the wall and fed it to one young.

These conflicts between nest building and feeding involved primarily the female. One time her mate arrived with insects that he fed to two nestlings. He then picked up some deer hair from the nest and fed it to one young. The fact that the female of this pair showed more ambiguous behavior than the male is probably related to the lead role female kinglets play in nest construction.

Which nestling gets fed first. Both parents tend to feed the nestlings that are the nearest to them. In 294 feeding visits made by both parents at one nest, the nearest nestling was fed first 123 times, the farthest nestling was fed first 56 times, the middle nestlings were fed first 46 times, and a random feeding occurred 69 times.

When the nestlings are between 10 and 13 days old they respond to the approaching call notes of their parents and "tsip" excitedly. They also stretch up and over the edge of the nest in the direction of the approaching parent. The ones nearest to the parent at that moment get fed first. Since the parents seldom vary the direction from which they approach the nest, the same ones tend to get their fill before the other hungry young have their turns. Because the nestlings do shift nest positions frequently, all young eventually get fed.

In one nest after the male disappeared and the female had assumed the exclusive role of feeding nine nestlings, the runt of the litter was crowded over to the opposite side of the nest from the approaching female and was seldom fed. Once it received no food for over a 3½ hour period. It starved two days later and was pushed to the nest bottom and trampled underfoot by the other nestlings. While the male was around to help feed the nestlings, the female was observed digging the runt out from the bottom of the nest two times when it was 2 days old, twice at 5 days, and once when it was 8 days old. After the male disappeared, the female fed the ones nearest to her every time.

Nest sanitation. During the early part of their nestling period, young kinglets usually defecate just after they have been fed. Both parents showed great impatience if there was any delay and gave a series of call notes. On one occasion the male finally seized a nestling's posterior and squeezed out the fecal sac.

Both adults swallow most, if not all, fecal sacs until the nestlings are 3 to 4 days old. Ornithologists report that when first hatched, a nestlings' digestive system is not too well developed. Undigested food passes through their systems; thus, the fecal sacs may provide some food value to the parents.

When the nestlings are 5 days old, some sacs are eaten, but most are carried off. No adult was observed eating fecal sacs after the youngest nestling was 6 days old. By this age, the nestlings are able to digest most of their food.

After 6 days nestlings void at any time; consequently, the

An adult kinglet about to carry off a fecal sac. Both parents eat most of the fecal sacs when the nestlings are 3 to 4 days old.

adults fall behind in nest sanitation, and the fecal sacs tend to pile up in and around the nest. Sanitation is especially a problem for single parents. The female that lost her mate before the nestlings fledged was unable to keep up with sanitation, and many sacs accumulated in, outside, and on the surrounding branches immediately below the nest.

The urge to keep the nesting area clean is generally quite strong. However, if none of the nestlings voids after a feeding visit, both adults continue to carry off the old fecal sacs outside the nest and on the branches below the nest. When nestlings voided over the side of the nest while a parent was feeding, the adult would often fly off and catch the sac in midair.

At one nest the nestlings, who were 4 to 7 days old, defecated 79 times in a 16-hour period. The adults ate 72 sacs and removed 7. Most of the fecal sacs were eaten at the nest or in the nest tree. Some were also carried to nearby trees and eaten there. Other sacs were carried off and dropped; this was followed by a vigorous bill-wiping session on a tree limb.

Ectoparasites. Nestlings in all nests under study appeared to harbor ectoparasites barely visible to the naked eye. Both parents usually noticed the parasites while they were waiting for a nestling to defecate, picked them off, and ate them. Peters (1936) lists one louse and one fly as external parasites of the golden-crowned kinglet found in the eastern United States.

Nestling food. During the nesting cycle kinglets gather food by foraging almost exclusively among spruce, fir, and pine branches. Using forceps, we removed samples of insects from the bills of a number of adult kinglets before they were able to feed their nestlings. These samples were submitted to entomologist Alvah Peterson for identification.

Among the insects were both adult and larval forms of

moths and butterflies. These included hairstreaks, canker-worms, cabbage loopers, Ilia underwings, and cutworms. Adults also fed the nestlings lacewings, crane flies, midges, hover flies, caddis flies, mosquitoes, aphids, tree hoppers, book and bark lice, tree bugs, leaf bugs, plant bugs, web spinning and leaf rolling sawflies, Harlequin cabbage bugs, and ladybird beetles. Both long- and short-legged spiders also made up part of the nestlings' diet, along with small, coiled snails.

The food collected from kinglets in late June during the first nesting period differed decidely from that of the second brood in late July. The kinglets must have been collecting what was readily available.

When one female shared feeding duties with her mate, she brought in tiny winged and wingless insects, larvae, and an occasional moth. After he disappeared, she brought primarily large daddy longlegs and moths. Perhaps these were the food items that were most abundant and readily available close to the nest.

Adult food. When nestlings did not respond, the parents occasionally ate the food that they had brought. After the eggs hatch, adults have such a strong innate urge to feed their gaping nestlings that they collect most insects that are available. When they no longer have the gaping mouths to worry about, they are more selective in gathering food for themselves.

Information on what adult kinglets eat before and after the nesting cycle is scanty. I know of only two other records in which actual food items were examined; both were from the stomachs of birds that had been shot. In the first, King (1883) examined the stomach contents of nine kinglets from Wisconsin. Two had eaten small flies; three, small beetles; one, caterpillars; one, a small chrysalid; and three, very small fragments of unidentifiable insects. In the second account, small beetles were the sole item found in the stomachs (Beal 1907).

In addition to these analyses, some interesting observations have been made of kinglets feeding. Needham (1909) found kinglets entangled in hooks on several clumps of ripening burdock heads. He noticed insect larvae of two species present in considerable number on the burdock heads. Most abundant were the seed-eating larvae of an obscure little moth, *Metzgeria lapella,* the larvae of the burdock weevil were also present. Most of the birds captured were young, and Needham guessed that they were attempting to get the larvae. Skinner (1928) saw kinglets during the winter in North Carolina hunting the open blossoms of trees and shrubs to prey on the small insects attracted by flowers. Quite often the birds looked over the bases of pine needle bunches for the tiny insects that hid there. The only record of golden-crowned kinglets eating vegetable matter was by Skinner, who observed one taking bites from persimmon fruits. Apparently kinglets subsist almost entirely on animal matter.

A few other observations have been reported on kinglets feeding. They have been seen eating locusts in Nebraska (Henderson 1927), aphid eggs in Massachusetts (Forbush 1907), and small insects picked from thickened maple sap in Wisconsin (Francis Zirrer in Bent 1949). Adults must surely eat the same types of food that they feed their young. If we can assume this, we have an accurate record of some of the food they consume during the nesting period of their young.

9

Nestling Development

MANY BIRDS ARE BORN with down or small soft feathers, while others are naked. Kinglets are completely naked when they hatch, except for tufts of down above the eyes and on the crown. They are about the size of a bumblebee and have flesh-colored skin and yellow bills with orange-colored mouths.

The following record of development is a composite and generalized description of young from all observed nests.

On the day on which kinglets hatch, they have very little muscular control or coordination. They respond to adult feeding visits by raising their bills in one continuous motion from a horizontal to vertical position, then back to a resting or sleeping position. Adults jar the nest and give call notes to get a response to food. Young defecate primarily while their posteriors are in a horizontal position. At this age the nest-

Nestling on the day it hatched.

lings spend most of their time sleeping and make only slight wing and foot movements. Raising their heads to accept food seems an effort, and they appear unable to hold their heads in a fixed position for more than a fraction of a second. After feeding, young often fall on their sides or backs, then struggle feebly back to a prone position. Their eyes are completely closed, and they make no sound.

On day 1 kinglets sleep all of the time when not being fed. They accept food generally with their bills slightly above a horizontal position. One-day-old kinglets have very little head control. Head movement is wobbly; in fact their heads appear too heavy for their bodies. Wing movement is slight. They still lose their balance, toppling over after being fed. They attempt to back up to the nearest nest wall to defecate and aim their posteriors toward the rim. There is no sign of feather tracts, and no sounds are emitted. Total length is an inch.

At 2 days we heard kinglets make their first sound, a barely audible "tseek." There is little change in motor coordination, and their movements are primarily for food and defecation. They can hold their heads in a raised position momentarily but often fall on their backs after feedings. Movement of feet and wings is quite feeble. Their eyes are closed, and they sleep constantly. Traces of feather tracts appear on their wings and dorsal sides, but they remain naked ventrally.

At 3 days kinglets gape vertically on most feeding visits, but they must still be prodded or shaken to respond. They raise their posteriors slightly above a horizontal level when defecating. Eyes remain closed. By now the young are "tseeking" a little louder. Traces of sheath development can be seen on their heads, necks, legs, and sides of rear, and feather tracts on their wings and backs are beginning to darken. Nestlings are still naked ventrally.

Three-day-old nestling.

CHN
1975

Four-day-old nestlings make sounds like tiny hiccups. Traces of eye openings appear. Head movement is improved a little, but young still raise and drop their heads without much control. Most movements are still associated with food and defecation. When defecating, nestlings raise their posteriors vertically and toward their parents by moving their feet backwards and partly up the nest side. The dorsal feather tract now shows heavy darkening. Ventral sides are still naked except for traces on the lateral lines. Darkening appears on the upper and lower wings and head.

At 5 days eye slits are a little wider. The young are responding more for food when their parents land on the nest edge, and they show better control of their heads when feeding. Little movement takes place other than during feeding visits. At this age three lines of darkening are visible: one on each side of the crown as well as traces at the superciliary line. The dorsal feather tract is darker than at 4 days, with the central portion being the darkest and widest. Signs of sheath development appear on the wings.

Five-day-old nestling.

CHN
1975

On the sixth day nestlings' eyes are about one-eighth open. "Tsipping" sounds, though still weak, are audible at a foot or more. The young raise their heads with better control and hold them in position longer. Between feedings they remain low in the nest and during feedings they show no wing movements. The young begin to preen but with very little control. They can beat their wings synchronously several times; however, they spend most of their time sleeping. A trace of sheath development appears at the upper bends of their legs. Sheaths are developing on their primaries and secondaries, and traces of sheaths can be seen on the upper parts of their legs.

By 7 days a further increase in eye openings is visible. The 7-day-old nestlings preen more and can extend their feet under their wings to scratch their heads. They tend to defecate toward the adults. "Tsipping" sounds are still quite weak when they are being fed. There are no tracts with feathers out of the sheaths.

Seven-day-old nestling.

Eight-day-old nestlings respond to the movements of one another and to the approach and departure of the adults by gaping. By now their eyes are about one-third open. Between feeding visits they spend most of their time sleeping. When not sleeping, they preen more often than they did at 6 or 7 days old. They "tsip" while being fed, and they are able to beat their wings low in the nest. Their stomachs remain naked, while centers of their crowns are becoming darkened.

Seven- to 9-day-old nestlings. Note difference in eye opening.

At 9 days nestlings' eyes are about one-half open. Much "tsipping" takes place while they are being fed. When their parents approach, the nestlings respond by gaping and continue to "tsip" after their parents depart. They also gape at one another's wing movements more often. When removed from the nest, they crawl forward. They continue synchronous wing beating, but these movements are still not strong. They are able to stretch full length for the first time. Preening activity increases but is still quite awkward. Feathers first appear out of the sheaths on their primaries, secondaries, and retrices.

Nine-day-old nestling.

CHN
1975

By day 10 the eyes of the young are about three-fourths open. They sense the approach of their parents at greater distances from the nest, "tsipping" continuously with gaping bills in the direction of the approaching adult. They crawl awkwardly in the nest and do more scratching and preening.

At 11 days their eyes are completely open. They crawl backward and up the nest wall to defecate onto the rim of the nest or into a parent's bill. Preening is more controlled, vigorous, and frequent. Feathers have broken out of the sheaths on all tracts. Nestling length is now nearly 2 inches.

Twelve-day-old nestlings beat their wings often, do more crawling about in the nest, and sit or stand on top of one

Eleven-day-old nestling.

CHN
1975

another so they are in two tiers. They are fairly adept at preening all parts of their bodies.

At 13 days nestlings respond to other bird songs and nearby sounds by "tsipping" and gaping in the direction of the noises. They spend less time sleeping and more time gaping at one another's movements and beating their wings and preening. By now feathers on their primaries are about one-third of an inch long—twice what they were at 11 days. At this age we stopped measuring feather lengths for fear of causing premature fledging.

Thirteen-day-old nestling.

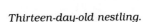

CHN
1975

No clearly definable advances were noted at 14 days.

At 15 days the nestlings crawl over one another, and generally stack themselves in two to three tiers. They do much wing beating. By now the nest is very crowded. The young do more cowering at noises or at movements in our blind. They are very alert, reacting quickly to the approaching "tsee" calls of the adults by creating a din of "tsipping" and extending their gaping bills well out of the nest toward the adults.

When nestlings sense the approach of a parent, they gape in the direction of the adult and maintain a din of "tsipping."

Nestling Development

Fifteen-day-old nestling.

CHN
1975

Nestling Development

When nestlings are 15 days old, they have just about outgrown their nest and are stacked in two or three tiers.

At 16 days the young peck at one another. There is less "tsipping" and more cowering at sounds in the immediate nesting area. They crawl out into the surrounding twigs and up to a foot from the nest, returning quickly, and perch on the nest rim for short periods. Between feedings they may take brief naps, sleeping with their bills and parts of their heads on their backs or under their wings.

Nestlings begin to crawl out of the nest a foot or so when they reach 16 days of age.

This 19-day-old nestling has crawled out on a limb and is ready to fledge.

Seventeen-day-old nestlings are very attentive to the movements of one another. They peck at and seemingly try to devour one another's bills or wing tips. They are also attentive to insects that fly around the nest, following insect flight movements with their heads and "tsipping" incessantly. They crawl in and out of the nest more often and do much preening, scratching, and stretching.

At 18 to 19 days nestlings perch more frequently on the nest rim, often crawling out on the branch supporting the nest where they preen and beat their wings. Their tail feathers are not too well developed, which makes them look tailless. Just before they fledge at 18 or 19 days, there is much crawling or hopping to and from the nest. Adults feed them in and around the nest, tending to favor those still in the nest.

Nestling weights. Of nestling weights we recorded, five nestlings in one nest more than doubled their average hatching weights by the second day. On the third day this nest was raided by a predator, so we were unable to get further weights. Three nestlings weighed at a second nest gained from five to seven times their hatching weights by the seventh day, at which time they averaged 0.18 of an ounce. The one that was the lightest when hatched, surpassed the weight of the nestling that was the heaviest by the seventh day after hatching. No nestling at this nest was weighed after the ninth day. We stopped weighing nestlings about halfway through their nestling cycle for fear of triggering premature fledging.

10

Fledging

FLEDGING IS THE PERIOD when kinglets have acquired the necessary feathers for flight. Golden-crowned kinglets usually leave the nest between 16 to 19 days after hatching. The earliest fledging ages we observed were between 14 and 16 days after hatching. Most of these apparently fledged prematurely because only three of the eight survived their first day out of the nest. Five were unable to fly well enough to remain in the trees.

In a second brood of a pair the nestlings fledged early—when they were 15 to 16 days old. Until the oldest members were 9 days old they were taken from the nest daily to check weight and feather tract development, and later, at 14 days, they were all removed individually for experiments. (These are described in Chapter Eleven.) Perhaps removing them from the nest so late in the nestling cycle triggered an earlier than normal departure. The nestlings of this pair's first nest did not fledge until they were 18 to 19 days old. They were not handled as much as those in the second nest or as late in the nestling period. Since 61 percent of all the 46 fledglings we recorded were between 18 and 19 days old, we feel this length of time is closer to the normal duration for the nestling period.

As already noted, nestlings usually crawl to and from neighboring twigs and branches a foot or two away for several days before leaving permanently. After the first young leave the nest, a chain reaction follows: within minutes the remaining nestlings leave the nest. In the six nests where nestlings were observed to fledge, the shortest time for the nest to empty was 15 minutes; the longest, 105 minutes. All young fledged before noon, the earliest at 6:40 A.M. and the latest at 11:57 A.M. One nestling was startled and flew several yards to a neighboring tree from a nest in late afternoon, just as I moved a branch to expose the nest for observation. However, the following morning that bird was back in the nest with the other nestlings.

Fledgling behavior. When the young leave the nest, they usually fly horizontally to a tree 10 to 15 feet away, where they squat, "tsipping" incessantly. This calling is ef-

This pair of young has just fledged. They located one another by their "tsips" and are awaiting their parents' arrival.

fective in locating one another and is usually done within two hours. They then gather on the same limb in a tight row, spending most of their time preening between feeding visits by their parents. One brood of seven we watched for three hours spent the entire time pressed together on the same perch.

Fledglings remain within 4 or 5 feet of each other for the first 3 to 4 days after fledging. They can easily be located within their territory because they generally perch on the same limb (about 30 feet or more from the ground) and they almost constantly "tsip" while waiting to be fed. It is a wonder that they survive their fledging period because it seems only natural that their constant calling would attract predators.

Whether one or both parents feed the fledglings depends on the stages of fledging and nesting. During the short time after some of the young have left the nest but others are still in it, both parents split feeding duties, favoring the nestlings with more feeding visits. Only on the first day out of the nest do both adults continue to feed the fledglings of their first brood. Thereafter, feeding is done almost exclusively by the male because the female has begun incubating in her second nest. Periodically, the male leaves his fledglings and feeds his mate while she incubates at the second nest. She seldom visits the fledglings but may forage for food nearby. About the time the fledglings in the first nest can take care of themselves, the eggs in the second nest hatch. After this second brood fledges, both parents share almost equally in feeding them.

Feeding trips made to fledglings are almost twice the number that are made to nestlings. During the nestling period young are fed an average of 12 to 14 times per hour with feeding visits split fairly evenly between parents. Fledgling young from the first brood, on the other hand, are fed entirely by the male an average of 24 times per hour. This difference is due in part to the aggressiveness of the young in begging for food and the distance from the nest the parent travels to gather food. As the young get older, the male collects food near them and feeds them while they are looking over his shoulder for more. The young also chase after him in pursuit of food.

Persistence of the young is probably the reason for another difference after fledging—the number fed per trip. On each feeding trip to young in the nest, parents fed three young per visit. After fledging, however, the male rarely fed more than one young per visit.

While attending the fledglings, the male is very alert to nearby activities of predators such as red squirrels. One red squirrel that climbed a tree about 30 feet from fledglings 12 days out of the nest was quickly confronted by the male kinglet. He approached to within 3 feet of the rodent, giving strident, single call notes. The squirrel ran down the tree only to climb another one a little farther from the fledglings and was accompanied closely by the distressed parent. The squirrel climbed to the crown of that tree and fed on cones. After about two more minutes of strident calling the male returned to his feeding duties. The squirrel did not appear to pay too much attention to the fledglings.

As the number of days out of the nest increases, noticeable changes in fledgling behavior take place. About the fifth day out of the nest the young begin to anticipate the approaching adult, and they make begging movements in his direction while he is 60 to 70 feet distant. They also make their first attempt to forage on their own by pecking in the foliage and on the bark. They separate from one another more often but still come together and remain together most of the time. In flight they still look tailless and ungainly when compared to the adults, and they land ungracefully after taking short flights. Flights are restricted to about 10 to 15 feet. The young may scatter frantically when a different species of bird suddenly appears or lands above them. Generally, when this occurs, each takes flight to neighboring trees, lands in a heap, and while teetering on a limb or twig, tries to regain its balance and seeks a more comfortable perch.

After the fifth day there is an increase in calling, not only among the fledglings but also between them and the adults. This calling appears to make it easier for the fledglings to keep track of the adults and for the parents to find the young now that they are no longer in a convenient, close-knit group near the nest. The "tsipping" of the fledglings has become almost like the "tsees" made by adults but not quite so clear. The first signs of warbling take place, but the "tsees" and warble run together.

By the seventh day the fledglings are taking longer flights of up to 75 feet from one another, and are spreading out more in different trees before flying back and greeting one another. A stationary fledgling generally greets the return of another by gaping, fluttering its wings, and begging for food. They may also occasionally do this when other birds fly above them. They are seen more in pairs, rather than all clustered on the same limb. When a parent arrives with food, they fly to it amid a din of "tsipping" and follow it around, begging for more food even after the adult has fed them. They can give up to five call notes in succession, but the calling is more rapid and not so clear as the calls made by the adults. Their flights from one tree to another are rather erratic, tending to be indirect and circular even when not tracking the parent.

Between the eighth and eleventh day out of the nest the amount of foraging on their own increases; they spend more time accompanying the adult while it forages for their food. Some precede the parent along a branch while others follow, keeping up a constant din of call notes and begging for food. They peck at spruce needles and hover hummingbirdlike at the ends of twigs. They still appear quite clumsy while flying or landing and spend much of their time preening.

Although by this time the fledglings are beginning to fly and forage further from the nest, they still remain relatively close. For the first 11 days out of the nest, one family was always located within 380 feet from the nest site each day.

Fledglings between 12 and 16 days out of the nest gather a good deal of food for themselves but still energetically pursue the adults for food. Their tails are sufficiently developed so that they are capable of hovering in midair and maneuvering in flight almost as well as the adults.

No feeding visits by the parents were observed after the

young had been out of the nest 16 to 17 days. Apparently by this age they have reached full independent status.

Territorializing during the fledgling period.

Up to about 8 days out of the nest fledglings were never observed outside the territorial boundaries set up by the adult male, even though the young may wander up to 400 feet from their old nest.

After one family of fledglings had been out of the nest for 8 days, they drifted beyond the area that the male had consistently restricted to himself over the previous weeks. The habitat adjacent to the male's territory was a large semiopen area, bordered by alders and covered primarily by second-growth black spruce and tamarack with a few scattered aspen. All seven fledglings flew about 25 yards into this area. The adult first flew to a black spruce on the edge of his territory and gave three call notes. Two fledglings flew back to him; he fed one of them and wiped his bill vigorously on a limb. The others returned with a din of "tsipping," and the adult flew deeper into his own territory, followed by his pursuing fledglings. On the ninth day out of the nest the male engaged in a territorial song battle with a neighboring male kinglet. A short while later a brood of six fledglings accompanied by a nonsinging male came into this territory. The male whose territory was invaded paid little attention to them and went about feeding his own fledglings.

Territorial boundaries were also ignored by another kinglet, a single adult female. This bird was not observed to leave the territory that had been set up by her missing mate until the fifth day past fledging, and for the next three days we were unable to locate her or her brood. We found them again on the eighth day approximately 1,100 feet to the west of their nesting site. On the ninth day we found a family of five fledglings with one adult in the female's old territory. However, she was again feeding her three young approximately at the same location we had seen her the previous day. On the twelfth day out of the nest one of her fledglings disappeared. The female remained outside of her former territory with her two remaining fledglings until the young were 17 days out of the nest, after which they were never again seen together.

The singing and displaying of territorial defense ceases after the nestlings of the second brood fledge, making it more difficult to locate the adults each day because they no longer remained in their original nesting territory.

Bathing. We observed one fledgling taking a bath in the wet foliage of a cedar branch. It rolled from side to side, lost its balance, fell off, flew back, and continued its bathing on the moisture-ladened leaves.

Postjuvenile molt. None of the fledglings we observed had yet started their postjuvenile molt. According to Ridgway (1904) this is the predecessor of the first winter plumage. After completing this molt young kinglets acquire their distinctive crown patch colors and are practically indistinguishable from adults. Although Ridgway says the postjuvenile molt begins early in August, none of the fledglings at Itasca had begun to molt before August 22, the latest that we observed them in the area. Unfortunately, due to my teaching responsibilities, we were unable to remain in our study area until the kinglets migrated.

11

Experiments

RARELY DOES MAN get the opportunity to come into contact with wild birds, but if he does, it is because they are either sick or injured. The success rate for nursing such birds back to good health is extremely low. Nature has a law about the survival of the fittest: The weak shall perish, and the strong shall survive.

Noodnik. From one of the nests we were watching, six of seven nestlings fledged and collected in a black spruce about 20 feet away. The one that remained behind perched on a limb a few feet below the nest. Both adults continued to feed this flightless bird along with the others over a period of six hours. But when it tried to fly, it ended up on the ground, and its intermittent "tsips" brought no response from the parents.

After the bird was ignored by adults for over an hour, I picked it up from its grounded position, since I feared that the ever-present red squirrels would find it before long. The fledgling failed to respond to insects that we presented to him at the site, so we took it to our cabin and put it in a kinglet's nest that we had collected earlier. We named him Noodnik.

Noodnik is perched on Carlyn's finger. He had fledged prematurely and was abandoned by his parents when he ended up on the ground.

Noodnik survived the night and greeted us with "tsip-ping" notes early the next morning. He gaped when I wiggled my finger in front of his bill, so I quickly waved an insect net through the grasses outside our cabin and netted a variety of insects. We were able to feed him his fill by wiggling a finger a few inches from him, and then stuffing insects into his bill from the side with our forceps.

He did not like to be left alone, and he followed us around the cabin constantly. When either of us sat down, he would crawl up a handy pant leg, work his way to shoulder level, and huddle against the nearest neck.

Later in the morning we put him in a small cardboard box, took him to the northeast boundary of the park, and climbed to our tree platform to introduce him to another female kinglet we were studying. We selected this parent because her nest was next to an existing platform. Other nests we were studying had to be reached by our using spikes to climb the nest tree. We couldn't observe the parents in these nests as well, and transporting Noodnik up to one of these nests would have been more difficult.

The female we chose was incubating high in a black spruce. We set Noodnik in his box next to her nest. When Noodnik saw her, he "tsipped" immediately, fluttered his wings, and begged for food. The adult crested, cocked her head, hopped on the box, picked up an insect that was in the box, and flew off. She returned in a couple of minutes with a tiny larva and, to our joy and relief, fed Noodnik. In 10 minutes she had made seven additional feeding visits to him, delivering extremely tiny insects. We held two moths toward her. She ate both of them and then flew off. She made eleven more feeding visits to Noodnik in 30 minutes. The male followed her to the nest on one of these visits. When he saw Noodnik, he gave three rapid call notes, crested, and flew off.

The female made several more feeding trips to Noodnik before settling down to incubate her eggs. Noodnik fluttered onto the nest and then hopped on top of her just as the male arrived with some large insects. Noodnik begged for them and was promptly fed. The female left. When she returned, Noodnik was standing on her eggs. She hopped into the nest and squeezed him to one side as she poked her bill into the bottom of the nest and turned over some eggs. It was an extremely tight fit for both of them and Noodnik popped out on top.

She made no attempt to attack the fledgling, but she did display frustration by digging into the nest and moving the eggs about in an effort to get them into her brood pouch. I prodded her off the nest, but she returned immediately and continued her efforts to get down on the eggs. I measured the temperature around the eggs, and it was a low 91°F. After more egg rolling and digging into the nest the temperature dropped another degree, so I removed Noodnik. The female settled down on the eggs and within three minutes heated them up to 102°F—a temperature high enough for incubation.

It was quite interesting to see that the male persisted in collecting large insects and feeding them to Noodnik, but the female brought extremely tiny items and appeared to feed him by regurgitation. The male had just completed his feeding responsibilities with the fledglings from the first nest, who were now independent, so he was used to collecting large insects for them. However, the female was incubating the second clutch of eggs and seldom visited her first fledglings.

Noodnik voided once when the female was present; she ate his sac and remained on the nest. I had never seen adults eat the fecal material of nestlings after they were six days old.

With misgivings, we put Noodnik back in his box and returned with him to our cabin.

The following morning we returned to Noodnik's territory and located his real parents and the other fledglings who were being fed about 35 feet up in a spruce. Noodnik began "tsipping" inside the box. When the adult male heard him, he flew to a limb about 5 feet above the box. When I opened the box, Noodnik flew out, landed on the ground, ran to a tamarack tree about 5 feet away and worked his way up to a limb about 10 feet above the ground. Then he flew to three different tamarack trees, maintaining a flight level of about 15 feet above the ground. He finally worked his way up to a branch about 22 feet from the ground. The male fed him six times, and the female made one visit. However, Noodnik eventually ended up on the ground where he was no longer fed, so again we took him back to our cabin.

The next day we went back to the north boundary and presented him again to the same incubating female to whom we had introduced him two days earlier. Noodnik begged for food; the female immediately left the nest and returned with insects. Noodnik was perched on my hand; the female landed on it and fed him. She flew off, returned within two minutes, fed him again while he was on my hand, then hopped onto her nest and continued incubating.

The male approached with some food, apparently for his mate, but she flew off. When Noodnik confronted the male with a gaping mouth, he fed him. The female returned shortly with tiny insects and presented them to her eggs with stamping and "tseeing." When she saw Noodnik, who was now perched on a branch above her nest, she flew to him, fed him, and returned to the nest. Both adults made several more feeding trips to Noodnik before we returned with him to the cabin.

Noodnik had appeared to gain in strength and was able to fly further each time he tried, but his flight patterns were almost horizontal or on a downward pattern. He did not tolerate being left alone and continuously perched on us or chased after us when we were in the cabin. He had completely adopted us as his parents.

I decided to record his voice, so I set him on a black spruce branch we had in the cabin. Suddenly he emitted a series of "tsips" and dropped from the branch to the floor.

When I held out my hand, he hopped onto it, huddled to one side of my cupped hand, and rolled over, dead. We kept asking, "Why did he die?" He appeared so healthy. Then it occurred to us that maybe an accident at the trading post caused his death. (He had been perching on Carlyn's shoulder while we bought groceries when suddenly he flew off and ran into a shelf of canned goods and ended up on the floor. He was momentarily stunned, but then he appeared to recover.) This was confirmed when I prepared him for mounting and saw that the front portion of his head had a massive blood clot.

We had watched Noodnik grow from the time he had come out of his egg and helped him struggle when he failed to fledge normally. For the next few days there was a great void in our lives as we continued to follow the survivors of his family.

Food experiments. During the incubation period of one female we were watching, we presented her with numerous insects (flies, mosquitoes, deerflies) that we killed inside the blind. The kinglet ate all of them.

After the eggs hatched, we continued to offer her insects as well as bits of food from our lunch. On the first day that the eggs began hatching, Carlyn held out a peanut while the female was brooding and incubating. She left the nest, fluttered before Carlyn's fingers, took the peanut—a huge object for her tiny bill—and flew off with it. She also ate a piece of bread, a small piece of banana, and one mosquito from the tip of my finger. She picked a small black beetle from Carlyn's finger and flew off with it but did eat seven crushed black flies right from Carlyn's hand.

The following day this female kinglet ate three insects that were held in front of her bill while she was brooding, and she flew to Carlyn's hand and ate a piece of chocolate cake that was being offered.

Carlyn pulled a hair from her head and extended it toward the bird, who promptly took it and put it in the bottom of the nest. She accepted another hair, also putting it in the nest.

On the third day after the eggs had hatched, a tiny piece of eggshell from a boiled egg was extended to her while she was brooding the nestlings; she ate it. She also accepted a blue-bottle fly but regurgitated it, flew to a nearby limb, wiped her bill on a twig, and returned to the nest.

When the young were four days old, she ate a small bit of pulp from a plum and then pecked at the plum seed that still had some pulp clinging to it.

Up to this point she had been eating almost all the fecal sacs of the nestlings, as well as most of the bits of food we gave her, "human" or not. However, this behavior changed when both parents began carrying off most of the fecal sacs. After that, the female also began to carry off most of the food we presented to her, dropping it at some distance from the nest.

This began when the nestlings were five days old. Carlyn gave the female a small green larva that she had collected from a twig above the nest. The kinglet took it and fed it to one of the young. But when she saw a piece of plum on Carlyn's finger, she flew into the blind, picked it off the finger, and flew off with it. She repeated this behavior twice more. The female also accepted two pieces of white bread but flew off with them.

On the sixth day after the young hatched, she took from our fingers a piece of banana, part of an eggshell, a bit of plum, and one mosquito. She carried all the items away.

Egg experiment. We did an experiment with a female kinglet to see how she would react if we suddenly removed all of her eggs from her second nest and placed them a few inches away in her first nest from which the nestlings had recently fledged. We had already collected the old nest from its original location and planned to place it on the same branch as the second nest.

The female was well acquainted with us because we had observed her through one complete nesting cycle and part (fourth day of incubation) of the second one. On the morning of the experiment the kinglet refused to leave the nest, so I took a plastic spoon and lifted her out. She flew off the spoon and immediately returned to her eggs, but I held my hand over the nest opening. She flew to the opposite rim of the nest, crept back under my arm and back onto the nest rim, cocking her head from side to side. Then she flew away.

I put her old nest so it touched her second nest and transferred the eggs. She returned in a few minutes and approached the two nests from below, following the typical spiraling pattern up the tree to just below the old original nest. She pulled a feather from its bottom and put it in her now empty second nest; then she removed a second feather from the old nest and flew away. She returned in a few seconds with the feather, landed below the nests again, made a spiraling approach to the old nest, bypassed it, hopped into her second nest, and tucked the feather into the bottom of it. Then she went through the motions of incubating the empty nest.

Apparently missing contact with eggs, she raised and lowered herself several times while circling to the right and then to the left; then she settled down to incubating the nonexistent eggs. She ignored her eggs in the first nest. The nest site seemed to be more important to her than the eggs. I was unable to prod her off the nest, so I removed her by hand and replaced the eggs. She accepted the move and stayed.

Nestling experiments. Leaving the two nests in position, I waited until seven days after the eggs hatched. I then transferred the nestlings back to the old nest while both adults were away.

The adult male was the first to return. His bill was loaded with insects. The nestlings, now in the first nest, responded to him by gaping in his direction and "tsipping." He completely ignored them and addressed the empty nest, emitting call notes while stamping on the nest's edge. After getting no response from the empty nest, he ate the food himself and flew away, although he must have been able to hear the nestlings "tsipping" only 6 inches away.

The female arrived within a few minutes and did the same thing as her mate, completely ignoring the begging nestlings. Each adult made two more feeding visits without feeding the young, attempting only to feed in the empty nest. I returned the young to their own nest.

Seven days later when the oldest nestlings were 14 days old, I repeated the above experiment. The female was the first one to perch on the empty nest this time. She stamped and "tseed," while cocking her head from side to side. When one nestling in the old nest called and begged for food, she stretched her neck toward it and fed it. She also fed a second young that gaped. The female returned a second time and again landed on the empty nest, stamping and giving call notes. The nestlings in the old nest heard her and again responded by begging for food, and she fed one of them.

The male arrived just as she departed; he landed on the rim of the empty nest, stamped, and gave three call notes.

This time, the nestlings in the old nest failed to respond. He continued to stamp and "tsee" at the new nest three more times before eating the food and flying off. Each parent made two more visits to the empty nest, moved as if to feed any young they might find there, and then settled for the real ones by stretching their necks the few inches they needed to feed them. When one of the nestlings defecated, the female took the fecal sac and carried it away.

Again, the nesting site seemed to be of initially greater importance to these two adult kinglets than the nestlings themselves. Neither of them landed on the nest that housed their young during the following two days that we kept the young in the old nest. They did, however, feed them from the nest in which the nestlings had hatched. Just a week earlier they had failed to feed their nestlings outside of their own nest on the six visits they made while the young were in the old nest. At 14 days the nestlings were very aggressive at feeding time—gaping higher and well out of the nest. Perhaps that was why they were then fed by the adults.

Latex owl experiments. The same kinglets were also subjected to experiments with a latex replica of an eastern screech owl. We wanted to see how the birds would react to this latex owl. Although we had never heard or seen a screech owl in kinglet territory, we didn't think that mattered. We felt the kinglets would see the latex model as just "an owl," and so they did.

The first experiment was when the nestlings were 6 days old. As the male approached with a large green larva, I held the owl at the blind opening, which was about 2 feet from the nest. The larva grabbed onto a limb near the nest, and the kinglet struggled to pull it loose. As he was freeing the larva, he saw the owl, immediately gave a series of strident call notes, crested, flew to a neighboring tree 10 feet away, hammered the larva on a branch, and ate it. Then he wiped his bill vigorously on the limb, flashing his crest and still calling.

Soon the female approached the nest, emitting the usual

"tsee" call notes. When she noticed the owl, she hovered hummingbird-fashion in front of it, crested, and flew to where the male was perched. Together they gave many strident call notes while raising and lowering their crown feathers, fluttering their wings, rapidly flicking their tails, and foraging in and out among the spruce foliage. When I imitated the hoot of a great horned owl, they became excited and flew to the nest. I threw the owl out of the blind; it landed on the ground 40 feet below. Within a few minutes they quieted down and continued with their normal routine, ignoring the fallen model.

When the oldest nestlings were 10 days, I put the same latex owl into a manila envelope with a slot, exposing only its eyes. When the female arrived at the nest to feed, she saw the eyes and flew off, visibly excited and emitting strident "tsee" notes. I hooted and threw the owl out of the blind, and it fell to the ground far below. The male joined his mate, and they flew off together into the nearby treetops greatly excited. She returned in three minutes, however, and fed her nestlings.

Twenty-four hours later I again repeated the experiment of exposing the owl in the envelope and tossing it to the ground as the female, closely followed by her mate, approached the nest with insects. She immediately gave single strident "tsees," fluttered in midair before the envelope, crested, and flew to a neighboring tree where she swallowed the insects, wiped her bill on a limb, and continued calling. This time the male seemed unconcerned over the entire episode. Possibly he had not seen the owl. He fed the gaping nestlings and joined her. The female's excitement rapidly subsided, and they both departed.

Great horned owl experiments. A different pair of kinglets was exposed to a stuffed, mounted specimen of another potential predator, a great horned owl. The owl was placed on the tree platform approximately 3 feet from and at the height of a nest containing nine nestlings. The owl was exposed to the adults on alternate feeding visits for a period of one hour.

The reaction to the horned owl was similar to the reaction to the latex screech owl. They crested, swallowed the loads of insects that were in their bills, flew to neighboring spruce trees, and appeared and disappeared among the twigs. Although they constantly emitted strident "tsee" notes, they continued collecting insects until their bills were stuffed, but they would not come to the nest.

When I slowly lowered the owl head first toward the ground, both parents descended to each succeeding lower limb of the nest tree, giving strident "tsee" notes. After the owl came to rest on its side at ground level, both parents flew off and continued their normal duties.

We presented the owl to them again the following day. They reacted as before, giving strident call notes and feeding rapidly in the neighboring trees. During the first four exposures they crested so that their crown color patches were spread to the superciliary lines and emitted rapid, strident call notes. However, each succeeding exposure to the owl seemed to elicit a less violent response. Starting with the fifth exposure, both parents ceased spreading their crests. Each succeeding exposure brought less strident "tsees" until the ninth exposure when they no longer crested and returned to a nearly normal calling level.

They started to come to the nest to feed young in the presence of the owl after the tenth showing. However, they were not completely relaxed. They would perch on the nest edge and look down into the nest while keeping the owl in view. After the fifteenth visit, they paid no attention to it at all.

An attempt to rescue a starving brood. After the male of one pair we were watching disappeared, the 14- to 16-day-old nestlings apparently fledged prematurely five days later. When flying to neighboring trees, their flight pattern was downward. Three of them could maintain a horizontal flight pattern for distances of only 6 to 10 feet. One could not fly at all and remained in the nest tree, fluttering its wings and dropping progressively to lower branches until it ended on the ground. Before long, four more fledglings became grounded from successive flights that carried them downward. We retrieved all grounded birds and returned them to the nest. Within a few minutes, they all left again and scattered among the nearby trees, only to become grounded again.

An hour later Carlyn found one climbing up the trunk of an aspen. It fell to the ground, climbed the tree again, and fell once more. She picked it up and put it with two of its brood mates on a fir limb about 6 feet from the ground. The female flew down and fed one. One of the fledglings tumbled off the limb and landed on the ground. It hopped over to the trunk and climbed part way up as the female arrived. She fed it again and departed. Within a few minutes all three fledglings fell from the branch to the ground.

Carlyn put them in a shoe box on the ground just as the female arrived to feed them. The female hovered over the box, flew off, returned, and flew off, only to return once more. She entered the box and fed one fledgling, flew to a spider web nearby, picked the spider off the web, and fed it to a fledgling perched in a fir tree about 8 feet from the ground.

We then captured all the young, including the three that could fly (the latter by shaking the tree until the fledglings fluttered gently to the ground onto the soft, furry moss). We put the eight birds in a shoe box. Then we took the three youngest of the brood and put them back on a fir bough. The female made 16 feeding visits to them within 30 minutes, gathering most of the food on low branches in nearby trees. Once, she foraged for food on the ground. When one fledgling fell to the ground, she continued feeding the two remaining on the limb but made no more feeding visits to the grounded youngster. At dusk we returned all the young to their nest.

The following morning the female made 3 visits to the nest before all the young left. The three fledglings that could fly perched in a fir about 16 feet above the ground. The others, however, became grounded. We located them by listening to their "tsipping" sounds. Two of them were extremely weak. When we put them on a limb, they fell and landed on the ground where they died. We tried to keep the

Once when the adult male arrived to feed the nestlings, I held the mirror about a foot from the nest. As soon as he saw his image, he fully crested, gave one loud "tsee" note, and flew off in the opposite direction of the mirror as though he had been struck by a bolt of lightning.

There was a definite learning process demonstrated by the kinglets during our experiments. The threshold for triggering a response became lower and lower as we exposed them to the same stimulus over and over.

remaining three alive in our cabin, but they also died
Perhaps the female was unable to rear such a large brood
without the help of the male parent, who had disappeared
four days before the nestlings fledged.

Mirror experiments.
When the oldest nestlings in
one nest were 15 days old, I put a hand mirror near the edge
of the nest. They responded by gaping toward it and keeping
up a constant din of "tsips." The experiment was repeated
several more times, and the nestlings always reacted the
same way.

*When we placed a mirror in front of the nestlings,
they reacted by gaping toward it and "tsipped"
continuously.*

12

Nesting Success

T HE MOST FREQUENT CAUSES of mortality among kinglets are predation, starvation, and faulty or infertile eggs. Starvation is linked to predation when both parents are killed while caring for nestlings or when one parent has to assume the feeding chores without aid from the other partner. It apparently takes the energies of both parents to raise a healthy brood.

Hatching and nestling success. If we include only nests that contained complete clutches of eggs, 10 nests with a total of 86 eggs were involved in our study. Of that total, 4 eggs disappeared, 1 egg in each of six clutches did not hatch, and 1 egg contained a dead young. The remaining 75 eggs hatched for a hatching success of 87 percent. Why a few eggs did not hatch or disappeared, one can only guess.

Eggs that did not hatch were not removed from the nest by the parents. The 4 eggs that were not accounted for may have hatched dead young who were removed by the parents. The cracked egg that contained a dead embryo was not removed during the two hours its contents were exposed; but when observations were resumed the following day, it was gone. Apparently kinglets remove dead nestlings, but not unhatched eggs.

In another nest when a 13-day-old nestling starved, the adult female made no attempt to remove it. However, it was doubtful that she knew it had died; the remaining 8 nestlings had outgrown the nest and spent most of the time standing in two or three tiers.

Survival of nestlings from hatching to fledging was also high. Out of 88 nestlings in 12 nests, 13 were taken by predators and 1 starved, leaving a nestling success of 84 percent.

Fledgling success. Of 74 nestlings that fledged, we were able to keep track of 30 from four different families. Twenty-four of these reached independence—a fledgling success of 80 percent.

Five young from one family died on the first day they fledged. They could not fly well enough to remain in the trees and were ignored by the adult female when they became grounded. The adult male had disappeared during the latter part of the nesting cycle. Starvation was believed to be the cause of their deaths. One of this family's 3 remaining fledglings disappeared on the twelfth day out of the nest, leaving 2 who reached the age of independence.

In addition to the four families that we followed until their young became independent, we tracked two others part of the way through the fledgling period. We followed one family for six days (6 fledged) and the other for eight days (9 fledged). Both families were still in their established territory when we ceased tracking them.

Predation. We never saw a predator find a kinglet nest and eat eggs or young. However, we have evidence that links the destruction of two nests to red squirrels and one nest to gray jays.

One of the nests that we believe was destroyed by a red squirrel had been lowered from 59 feet to 8 feet above the ground. Twice earlier during the incubation cycle we had rescued the nine eggs from red squirrels. Six days after eight of the nine eggs hatched, the nest was destroyed. The day before the nest contents disappeared, a red squirrel ran around the rim of a bucket that contained the cut portion of the tree base.

The second nest believed to have been destroyed by a red squirrel contained eight eggs. The following day when I checked to see if a ninth egg had been laid, the nest was empty; just 20 feet away were two red squirrels feeding on cones.

The pair whose nest was lowered from its original height almost lost their second brood of nine nestlings to red squirrels. We shot six squirrels just as they were about to enter a nest.

In another nest gray jays were the prime suspects in killing five of seven nestlings, the oldest being 16 days. As we were leaving our tree platform for the day, a flock of seven gray jays drifted into the area near the nest and were stalked by the adult kinglets. When we returned to the blind the next day, a dead young—with its viscera and right eye gone—was in the nest. On a limb 3 feet below the nest were two more dead nestlings, each with one eye and their viscera missing. A fourth nestling had been forced into a crack in the tree trunk 2 feet below the nest; only its wing tips were visible. A fifth nestling was discovered in the moss 57 feet below the nest, minus one eye and viscera. The last two escaped and were perched about 40 feet up in a spruce, where the parents were feeding them. Only a bird predator would be capable of pecking out the eyes or forcing a nestling into a tree crack.

In addition to predation on young, predation on adults was also suspected. Two nesting females and one male were thought to have been the victims of sharp-shinned hawks who were frequently seen in kinglet territories. One of these females, who was incubating nine eggs, remained on the nest while a sharp-shinned hawk perched just 15 feet from her. Five of her eggs were pipped and ready to hatch. When we returned the next day, there were nine cold eggs and no sign of the female. Her mate was singing a series of complex songs at the very tip of a black spruce nearby. He was seen in his territory the following four days, but the female was never seen again.

The other female suspected of being a hawk's victim had reared a brood of nine nestlings and had been incubating eight eggs in her second nest for about eight days. We did no further observation at her nest, but when we returned to collect the empty nest five weeks later, there were still eight eggs in it.

Nest desertion. Out of 19 nests under study there were three desertions; all were apparently due to our activities. I took motion pictures at one nest while the male and female were putting nesting materials into place during the fourth day of nest construction. The noise of the camera frightened the adults away, and they never returned. The second desertion took place after the seventh egg had been laid in a nest that we checked once or twice daily by climbing the nesting tree. Apparently, the parents never got used to our visits. This same pair deserted their second nest on the fifth day of nest construction, probably for the same reason they left their first one. We believe desertion is rare among kinglets not disturbed by human observers.

Mortality rates. It is difficult to get a true picture of golden-crowned kinglet mortality rates under natural conditions. One cannot observe a large number of these birds without first scaling the trees and parting the branches that hide the nests. Consequently, the first visit by man leaves a trail to the nest for a potential tree-climbing predator. Each successive climb leaves a more pronounced path.

One pair lost its nest to a predator after we had lowered it. The chances of red squirrels finding the nest were vastly increased because the only foliage on the tree was in the immediate vicinity of the nest, the area where red squirrels would most likely go to seek cones. We had removed all the remaining greenery.

Conversely, we protected eggs and nestlings from predators when the animals had found a nest or were in the vicinity of one. We also saved nestlings that had fallen through holes in two different nests.

Thus, our presence in the study area both invited and hindered nest destruction. In spite of this, hatching, nestling, and fledgling successes were remarkably high—80–87 percent. Why does a bird with such a low mortality rate double-brood? Why do they produce so many eggs with such a high rate of success? Why are not kinglets living in plaguelike numbers all through the Minnesota north woods?

We believe that the success of reproduction we observed is probably higher than what probably exists under natural conditions. We suspect that red squirrels, in Itasca, are the main predators of golden-crowned kinglets. If we had not partially controlled the numbers of these rodents in all areas under intensive study, we believe kinglet mortality would have been much higher.

13

Reflections

T HE STUDY HAS ENDED, and it is now 30 years later. As Carlyn and I look back at our adventures with the golden-crowned kinglet, we can't help but marvel at how a pair of such dainty little creatures could survive torrential rains, heat, strong winds, and predation; raise two large families; and then migrate up to 2,000 miles or more to their wintering grounds.

Although we banded 57 nestlings during the early part of our study, we have received no band returns. Nor did we see any bands on the birds during the years following our initial banding. We worked the same areas each year. It is highly unlikely that such a tiny bird would be noticed after it met its doom. Perhaps our banded birds who survived did not return to the areas we studied.

In looking back one can easily gloss over the hardships involved in such a study as ours. It required a great deal of perseverance and drive that taxed us at times. We climbed out of bed and were on the scene every morning at the break of dawn, and collectively spent 16 to 17 hours of unbroken observation periods in blinds at the nesting sites. Many more hours were spent by each of us tramping around the territories when we were not on duty at the nest under intensive study. Other nests also had to be checked.

When our birds under intensive study began their second nest, our endurance was stretched further because we didn't get a chance to relieve each other. One of us had to remain at the first nest while the other observed activities at the second. When the nestlings fledged in the first nest, one of us followed the fledglings around while the other one remained at the second nest.

We also had a financial hardship. Each of us spent the equivalent of approximately 240 eight-hour days observing the birds. All this time we were without financial support and had to rely on our meager savings. I was enrolled as a student at the biological station the first two seasons, but we did the last three years as independent researchers.

However, each season our hardships were soon forgotten after we located our first kinglets' nest and we were perched atop a tower or tree platform viewing these tiny interesting creatures from only inches away. Their total acceptance of us—and perhaps our role, so we thought, as their protector— was most gratifying. Unlike so many other researchers who have had to do their work from a distance or remain completely hidden and quiet, we were able to have a close, friendly, relaxed relationship with the subject of our study.

At first we thought we were dreaming when the kinglets came into our blind, landed on us, and allowed us to pick them up. We were equally surprised when they allowed us to dab them with identifying paint, weigh their young while they hopped around the scale, take food from their bills for analysis, and stroke the females while they were brooding or incubating. The birds had tremendous tolerance when we lowered several nests from their selected treetop sites to successively safer and more accessible levels nearer the ground. The most interesting time was when I lowered one nest 51 feet over a period of three days, and the adults still stayed with it.

This same tolerance enabled us to view the kinglets without the use of a blind. Weather permitting, we removed the blind and got a bird's-eye view of the treetops. This allowed us to observe other birds and tree and ground mammals that would have gone unnoticed.

All in all, the rewards of the fieldwork clearly outweighed

the drawbacks. We can say the same thing today.

With the benefit of hindsight we can see some things more clearly now. After going over the vast amount of notes that we took each season, we wonder whether we did not overstudy these kinglets. We gathered some of the same kinds of information several times. But episodes are rarely repeated precisely in nature, and duplications are never undesirable in science. In spite of this we undoubtedly focused too much on some topics and overlooked others.

Long days of observations shortened the time left over for planning. Was the trade-off worth it? We think so. Before our study not much reliable information existed about this species. Published reports were rather sketchy and incomplete. Most records were based on brief sightings while the birds were in migration or had landed to gather food.

Since we completed our study, we know of no one who has undertaken further research on the golden-crowned kinglet. In the mid-1970s, Haftron, a European ornithologist, studied the British goldcrest, a similar species in northern Europe. He used closed-circuit TV. In comparing his studies with ours, we can conclude that the two species have somewhat similar nesting cycles (see Galati and Galati 1985).

A review of the literature—old and new—tells us the same thing. What we learned at Lake Itasca using direct and, by modern standards, relatively unsophisticated techniques helped fill a knowledge gap about a bird that was, for the most part, unknown.

In addition to helping us realize this, hindsight makes us glad we did the work when we did. The study could not have occurred at a better time in our lives. We were both healthy, wide-eyed, and full of energy and curiosity. At our current stage in life we would not be able to handle the task. Carlyn can still hear the plaintive call of the kinglet, but I have been out of auditory communication with these birds for a dozen years.

To have heard and seen as many kinglets as we have is a privilege. Because of their tiny size and tinier voice, golden-crowned kinglets will probably never be called common birds of our backyards or gardens. Few—other than ornithologists and bird buffs—will notice these birds in their native haunts in the coniferous forests.

So to answer once again the oft-repeated question, "Why did you study such a silly little bird that most people have never heard about?" my answer is still, "Because it was there." While most people have never heard of it, it goes about its business as an ally of humans, sticking to an almost exclusively insectivorous diet, which includes leaf-eating larvae and plant lice that could destroy our forests.

That silly little bird allowed us to delve into its most intimate secrets. The resulting study was one of the most delightful and rewarding experiences of our lives.

We hope this book will offer incentives for other researchers to conduct studies on high-nesting songbirds and other creatures about which little is known. We also hope the book encourages other writers as well. Finishing it has taken a great load off our shoulders. After spending so many hours, days, and seasons on such an interesting bird, publishing only a short scientific treatise of our voluminous findings seemed a waste. We could not let at least the most interesting aspects of our study go unheard.

It goes to show that stories—if they are good ones—are timeless and worth telling.

APPENDIX

Common and Scientific Names of
Plants and Animals Mentioned in the Text

THE FOLLOWING REFERENCES were used as primary authorities for common and scientific names mentioned in this book: plants—Read (1987), mammals—Hazard (1982), birds—American Ornithologists' Union (1983), insects and spiders—Borror and White (1970) and Milne and Milne (1980), and molluscs— *The Audubon Society Field Guide to North American Seashells* (1981).

PLANTS

Alder, speckled (*Alnus rugosa*)
Arrowwood, downy (*Viburnum rafinesquianum*)
Ash, black (*Fraxinus nigra*)
Aspen, quaking (*Populus tremuloides*)
Birch, dwarf (*Betula pumila*)
   European (*Betula pendula*)
   paper (*Betula papyrifera*)
Blueberry, early low (*Vaccinium angustifolium*)
   Canada (*Vaccinium myrtilloides*)
Burdock, common (*Arctium minus*)
Cedar, northern white (*Tsuga occidentalis*)
Dogbane, spreading (*Apocynum androsaemifolium*)
Dogwood, red osier (*Cornus stolonifera*)
Elms (*Ulmus* spp.)

Fern, bracken (*Pteridium aquilinum latuisculum*)
Fir, balsam (*Abies balsamea*)
Grass, cotton (*Eriophorum* spp.)
Hemlock (*Tsuga candensis*)
Honeysuckle, American fly (*Lonicera canadensis*)
Juneberry (*Amelanchier humilus*)
Lichens (*Hypogymnia physodes* and *Parmelia sulcata*)
Mosses (*Brachythecium salebrosum*)
Oak, bur (*Quercus macrocarpa*)
Persimmon (*Diospyros virginiana*)
Pine, jack (*Pinus banksiana*)
    red (*Pinus resinosa*)
    white (*Pinus strobus*)
Sarsaparilla, wild (*Aralia nudicaulis*)
Spruce, black (*Picea mariana*)
    white (*Picea glauca*)
Tamarack (*Larix laricina*)
Willow, Bebb's (*Salix bebbiana*)

MAMMALS

Badger (*Taxidea taxus*)
Bear, black (*Ursus americanus*)
Chipmunk, eastern (*Tamias striatus*)
    least (*Eutamias minimus*)
Coyote (*Canis latrans*)
Deer, white-tailed (*Odocoileus virginianus*)
Otter, river (*Lutra canadensis*)
Porcupine (*Erethizon dorsatum*)
Raccoon (*Procyon lotor*)
Skunk, striped (*Mephitis mephitis*)
Squirrel, red (*Tamiasciurus hudsonicus*)

BIRDS

Chickadee, black-capped (*Parus atricapillus*)
    boreal (*Parus hudsonicus*)

Cowbird, brown-headed (*Molothrus ater*)
Creeper, brown (*Certhia americana*)
Crow, American (*Corvus brachyrhynchos*)
Cuckoo, black-billed (*Coccyzus erythropthalmus*)
Flycatcher, alder (*Empidonax alnorum*)
   great crested (*Myiarchus crinitus*)
   least (*Empidonax minimus*)
Gnatcatcher, blue-gray (*Polioptila caerulea*)
Goldcrest, British (*Regulus regulus anglorum*)
Grosbeak, rose-breasted (*Pheucticus ludovicianus*)
Grouse, ruffed (*Bonasa umbellus*)
Hawk, sharp-shinned (*Accipiter striatus*)
Jay, blue (*Cyanocitta cristata*)
   gray (*Perisoreus canadensis*)
Kinglet, golden-crowned (*Regulus satrapa*)
Nuthatch, red-breasted (*Sitta canadensis*)
   white-breasted (*Sitta carolinensis*)
Ovenbird (*Seiurus aurocapillus*)
Owl, barred (*Strix varia*)
   great horned (*Bubo virginianus*)
Parula, northern (*Parula americana*)
Phoebe, eastern (*Sayornis phoebe*)
Robin, American (*Turdus migratorius*)
Screech-owl, eastern (*Otis asio*)
Sparrow, chipping (*Spizella passerina*)
   song (*Melospiza melodia*)
   white-throated (*Zonotrichia albicollis*)
Thrush, hermit (*Catharus guttatus*)
Veery (*Catharus fuscescens*)
Vireo, red-eyed (*Vireo olivaceus*)
   solitary (*Vireo solitarius*)
Warbler, blackburnian (*Dendroica fusca*)
   black-throated green (*Dendroica virens*)
   golden-winged (*Vermivora chrysoptera*)
   magnolia (*Dendroica magnolia*)
   mourning (*Oporornis philadelphia*)
   nashville (*Vermivora ruficapilla*)
   pine (*Dendroica pinus*)
Wood-pewee, eastern (*Contopus virens*)

Wren, winter (*Troglodytes troglodytes*)
Yellowthroat, common (*Geothlypis trichas*)

INSECTS

Aphid (Aphididae)
Beetle, ladybird (Coccinellidae)
Bug, leaf (Miridae)
  plant (Miridae)
  tree (order or family unknown)
Cabbage bug, Harlequin (Hemiptera)
Cankerworm (Geometridae)
Cutworm (Noctuidae)
Deerfly (Tabanidae)
Fly (*Ornithoica confluenta*)
  black (Diptera)
  blue-bottle (*Calliphora vomitoria*)
  caddis (Tricoptera)
  crane (Tipulidae)
  hover (Syrphidae)
Hairstreak (Lycaenidae)
Hopper, tree (Membracidae)
Lacewing (Chrysopidae)
Locust (order or family unknown)
Looper, cabbage (Noctuidae)
Louse (*Philopterus incisus*)
  bark (Psocoptera)
  book (Psocoptera)
Midge (*Chironomus*)
Mosquito (Culicidae)
Moth (*Metzgeria lapella*)
No-see-um, biting midge (Heleidae)
Sawfly, leaf rolling (Pamphiliidae)
  web spinning (Pamphiliidae)
Underwing, Ilia (Noctuidae)
Weevil, burdock (order or family unknown)

SPIDERS

Daddy longlegs (Phalangida)
Spiders, long-legged (Arachnida)
  short-legged (Arachnida)

MOLLUSCS

Snail (Gastropoda)

REFERENCES

American Ornithologists' Union. 1983. *Check-list of North American birds.* 6th ed. Baltimore: American Ornithologists Union.

The Audubon Society Field Guide to North American Seashells. 1981. New York: Knopf.

Beal, F. E. L. 1907. Birds of California in relation to the fruit industry. *U.S. Department of Agriculture Biological Survey Bulletin,* no. 30, 84.

Bent, A. C. 1949. Life histories of North American thrushes, kinglets, and their allies. *U.S. National Museum Bulletin,* no. 196, 382–87.

Borror, D. J., and R. E. White. 1970. *A field guide to the insects of America north of Mexico.* Boston: Houghton Mifflin.

Brewster, W. 1888. Breeding of the golden-crested kinglet (*Regulus satrapa*) in Worcester County, Massachusetts, with description of its nest and eggs. *Auk* 5:326–27.

Church, C. 1927. Friendly kinglets. *Bird-Lore* 29:324.

Forbush, E. H. 1907. *Useful birds and their protection.* 161–63. Boston: Massachusetts State Board of Agriculture.

Friedmann, H. 1971. Further information on the host relations of the parasitic cowbirds. *Auk* 88:245.

Galati, B., and C. B. Galati. 1985. Breeding of the golden-crowned kinglet in northern Minnesota. *Journal of Field Ornithology* 56:28–40.

Haftron, S. 1978. Cooperation between male and female Goldcrest *Regulus regulus* when rearing overlapping double broods. *Ornis Scandinavica* 9:124–29.

Hansen, H. L., and D. P. Duncan. 1954. The management of Itasca State Park forest to meet recreational objectives. *Proceedings of the Society of American Forestry Meeting,* 123–25.

References

Hazard, E. B. 1982. *The mammals of Minnesota*. Minneapolis: University of Minnesota Press.

Henderson, J. 1927. *The practical value of birds*. New York: Macmillan.

King, F. H. 1883. Economic relations of Wisconsin birds. *Geology of Wisconsin* 1:441-610.

Marshall, W. H., and M. F. Buell. 1955. A study of the occurrence of amphibians in relation to a bog succession, Itasca State Park, Minnesota. *Ecology* 36:381-87.

Milne, L. J., and M. Milne. 1980. *The Audubon Society field guide to North American insects and spiders*. New York: Knopf.

Minot, H. D. 1877. *The land birds and game birds of New England*. 55-56. Boston: Salem Press.

Needham, J. G. 1909. Kinglets captured by burdocks. *Bird-Lore* 11:261-62.

Nice, M. M. 1954. Problems of incubation periods in North American birds. *Condor* 56:173-97.

Peters, H. S. 1936. A list of external parasites from birds of the eastern part of the United States. *Bird-Banding* 7:9-27.

Read, R. H., comp. 1987. Wisconsin vascular plants and DNR codes. Wisconsin Department of Natural Resources. Unpublished list filed at the Bureau of Environmental Analysis and Review, Madison, Wis.

Ridgway, R. 1904. The birds of North and Middle America. *U.S. National Museum Bulletin*, no. 50, Part 3, 700-705.

Roberts, T. S. 1936. *Birds of Minnesota*. Vol. 2. Minneapolis: University of Minnesota Press.

Skinner, M. P. 1928. *Guide to the winter birds of the North Carolina sandhills*. Albany, N.Y.: Science Press Printing Company.

Swedenborg, E. D. 1939. Summer birds of the Lake Vermilion region. *The Flicker* 11:4-16.

Wood, A. H. 1884. Tameness of the golden-crested kinglet (*Regulus satrapa*). *Ornithologist and Oologist* 9:62.

INDEX

References to figures are printed in **boldface type.**